TAO

TAO

its history and teachings

OSHO

Audio CD: TAO – Its History and Teachings, © & (P) 1978, 2009
Osho International Foundation, Switzerland

This book is compiled from various works by Osho which are based
on his daily talks to international audiences. All of Osho's talks have
been published in full as books, and are also available as original audio
recordings. See: OSHO Library at www.osho.com/library.

ISBN 13: 978-0-9844444-3-4

Picture acknowledgments
The publishers would like to thank Siddhena Ian Murray-Clark for the
images on pages 13, 17, 24T, 24B, 36L, 36ML, 36MR, 36R, 47, 71T, 71B,
89, 104L, 104M, 104R, 106L, 106ML, 106MR, 106R, 123, 139 and for the
drawings of Taoist masters on pages 29, 31, 33, 45, 55, 57, 63, 67, 79, 85,
87, 121, 141.
All other images are © Osho International Foundation.

Typeset by Bookcraft Ltd, Stroud, UK
Printed in Thailand

10   9   8   7   6   5   4   3   2   1

contents

tao: the great rebellion

Taoist masters only talk about "the Way." Tao means the Way—they don't talk about the goal at all. They say: The goal will take care of itself; you need not worry about the goal.

If you know the Way, then you know the goal, because the goal is not at the very end of the Way, the goal is all along the Way—each moment and each step it is there. It is not that when the Way ends you have arrived at the goal; each moment, wherever you are, you are at the goal if you are on the Way. To be on the Way is to be at the goal. Hence, Taoists don't talk about the goal, they don't talk about God, they don't talk about *moksha*, *nirvana*, enlightenment—no, not at all. Very simple is their message: You have to find the Way.

Things become a little more complicated when the masters say: The Way has no map, the Way is not charted, the Way is not such that you can follow somebody and find it. The Way is not like a superhighway; the Way is like a bird flying in the sky—it leaves no footprints behind. The bird has flown but no tracks are left to follow. The Way is a pathless path. It is not ready-made, available; you cannot just decide to walk on it, you will have to find it. You will have to find it in your own way; nobody else's way will do. Buddha has walked, Lao Tzu has walked, Jesus has walked, but their ways are not going to help you because you are not Jesus, and you are not Lao Tzu, and you are not Buddha. You are you, a unique individual. Only by walking, only by living your life, will you find the Way. This is something of great value.

That's why Taoism is not an organized religion—it cannot be. It is an organic religiousness, but not an organized religion. You can be a Taoist if you simply live your life authentically and spontaneously; if you have the courage to go into the unknown on your own, as an individual; if, not leaning on anybody, not following anybody, you simply go into the dark night not knowing whether you will arrive anywhere or whether you will be lost. If you have the courage, that choice is there. It is risky. It is adventurous.

Christianity, Hinduism, and Mohammedanism are superhighways: you need not risk anything—you simply follow the crowd. With Tao you have to go alone, you have to be alone. Tao respects the individual, not the society. Tao respects the unique, not the crowd. Tao respects freedom, not conformity. Tao has no tradition. Tao is a rebellion, and it is the greatest rebellion possible.

The Way is not like a superhighway; the Way is like a bird flying in the sky—it leaves no footprints behind.

the principles
of tao

Tao is one, but the moment it becomes manifest, it has to become two. Manifestation has to be dual: it cannot be singular. It has to become matter and consciousness; it has to become man and woman. It has to become day and night; it has to become life and death. You will find these two principles everywhere. The whole of life consists of these two principles, and behind these two principles is hidden the One. If you continue to remain involved in these dualities, in the polar opposites, you will remain in the world. If you use your intelligence, if you become a little more alert and start looking into the depths of things, you will be surprised—the opposites are not really opposites, but complementaries. And behind them both is one single energy: that is Tao.

道

the ultimate synthesis

Tao means transcendence—transcendence of all duality, transcendence of all polarity, transcendence of all opposites. Tao is the ultimate synthesis—the synthesis of man and woman, positive and negative, life and death, day and night, summer and winter.

HOW DOES THIS synthesis become possible? How does one grow into that ultimate synthesis? A few things have to be understood.

First, the principle of yin—the principle of femininity—is like a ladder between hell and heaven. You can go to hell through it or you can go to heaven through it; the direction will differ but the ladder will be the same. Nothing happens without the woman. The energy of the woman is a ladder to the lowest and to the highest, to the darkest valley and to the lightest peak. This is one of the fundamental principles of Tao. It must be understood in detail. Once it is rooted in your heart, things will become very simple.

It will be good to go into the symbolism of Adam and Eve. The world does not start with Adam, it starts with Eve. Through Eve, the serpent persuades Adam to disobey. The serpent cannot persuade Adam directly. There is no direct way to persuade the man; if you want to reach him, you must go through the woman. The woman functions as a medium for the serpent. On the other hand, when Christ is born, he is born of the Virgin Mary. The Christ child is born of virgin femininity, out of virgin yin. The highest enters through the woman. The lowest and the highest have both been expressed through the woman.

Adam means "red earth." God made Adam out of red earth. Adam is the principle of dust unto dust. The man is the outer principle, the principle of extroversion: the man is the physical body. Try to understand these symbols. The man is the physical body, and God created Eve out of man's physical body. Eve was something higher. First the man had to be created, then the woman. The feminine was more subtle, more refined—a greater synthesis. Eve was created out of a rib because she could not be created directly from the earth.

To understand these symbols, consider that you cannot eat mud, but you can eat apples—apples are on a higher plane. They come from the mud in the sense that the tree grows out of the mud—so the apple is nothing but earth transformed. You can eat

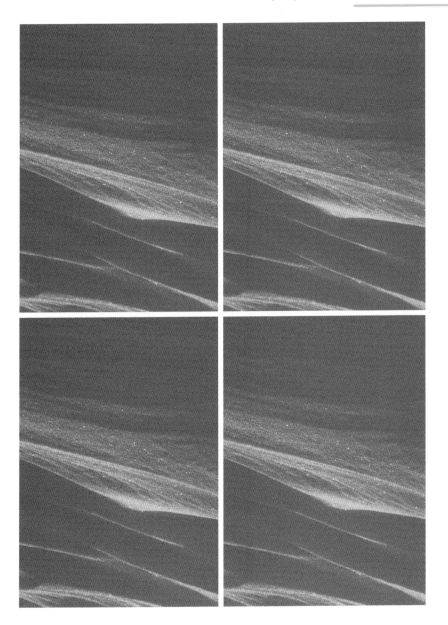

> *Tao has no tradition. Tao is a rebellion, and it is the greatest rebellion possible.*

the apple and digest it, but if you try to eat the earth, you will die. The apple is from the earth, but it is a superior synthesis—better tasting, more digestible.

God created Adam—and man has taken it to mean that because God created the man first, he *is* first. No, the man was created first because he is very close to the earth. Then the woman was created—and since she is not as close to the earth; she was created out of Adam as a higher synthesis.

The name *Eve* is also significant. *Eve* means "the heart." Adam means the earth and Eve means the heart. God told Adam to name things, so he named everything. When he came to name Eve, he simply said, "She is my heart—Eve." *Eva* or *Eve* can be further translated into modern jargon to mean the psyche. Man is the body principle; woman is the psychic principle. Man is body; woman is mind. Everything happens through the mind.

If you are to do something wrong, your mind has to be convinced first; if you are to do good, your mind has to be convinced about that first. Everything happens first as an idea, only—then can it be actualized.

Your body cannot be persuaded to do anything unless your mind is ready. Even if an illness enters your body, it enters through the mind. Anything that ever happens, happens through the mind.

The woman is the principle of the inner—not, certainly, of the innermost, but of the inner. She is in the middle. The innermost is called the soul, the outermost is called the body, and just between the two is the psyche, the mind.

> *Through Eve, Adam disobeyed.*
> *Adam followed Eve on this adventure*
> *into the world.*

That is the meaning of the whole parable of Adam and Eve. The serpent persuaded Eve since only the mind can be persuaded, convinced, seduced. Then the mind can persuade the body easily. In fact, the body follows the mind like a shadow. Once your mind has a thought, it is bound to be translated into actuality.

Through Eve, Adam fell. Through Eve, he was expelled from the garden of God. Through Eve came this great adventure we call the world. Through Eve, Adam disobeyed. Adam followed Eve on this adventure into the world.

The parable about Jesus is the same, with a different emphasis. Jesus is born to the Virgin Mary. Why a virgin? If you understand rightly, virgin means a mind that is absolutely pure, uncontaminated by thought. Thoughts are represented by the serpent because the ways of thoughts are serpentine. If you watch your own thoughts, you will understand. They walk without legs just like serpents; they wriggle within you. They are cunning and clever and deceptive— like the serpent. They hide in dark holes in your unconscious and whenever they have an opportunity they sneak up on you. In the night, in the dark night, they come out; in the daylight they hide. When you are alert, those thoughts disappear; when you are not so alert, they come out and start influencing you.

The Virgin Mary is a mind in meditation; Eve is a mind full of thoughts, full of serpents. Jesus enters into the world through the Virgin Mary, through purity, through innocence. Thought is cunning; thoughtlessness is innocent.

When you understand these beautiful parables, you will be surprised: We have not done justice to them. They are not historical facts; they are great metaphors of the inner being of man. Through Eve, Adam fell, and through the Virgin Mary, Jesus rose and entered again into the world of godliness.

One thing more. It is said that the sin of Adam was disobedience. God had said not to eat the fruit of a certain tree, the Tree of Knowledge— but the serpent persuaded Eve and Eve persuaded Adam. It was disobedience.

You will be surprised to learn the Hebrew meaning of the name Mary. The Hebrew word for Mary is *mariam*, which— means "rebellion." Through disobedience, Adam fell, and through rebellion, Jesus rose.

Disobedience means a reaction, going against, against God. Rebellion means negating the negative, going against the world, going against the serpents. Eve listened to the serpents and went against God. Mary rebelled against the serpents and listened to God.

Disobedience is political; rebellion is religious. Disobedience only brings disorder. Rebellion, real rebellion, brings a radical change in being—a 180-degree turn, a conversion.

But both Adam and Jesus happened through the feminine principle.

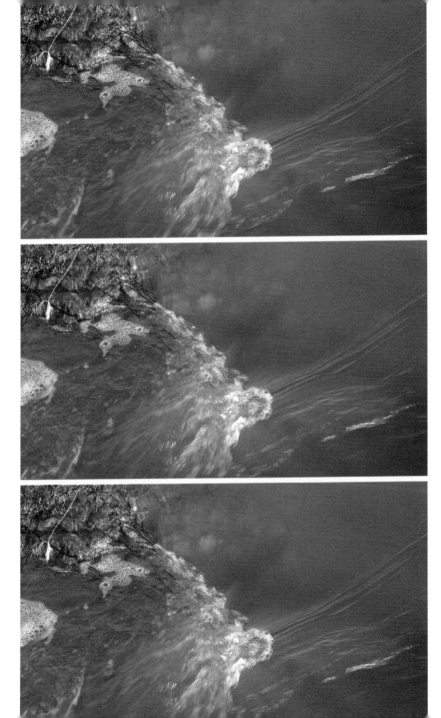

yin and yang

In Taoist language, the feminine principle is called yin and the male principle is called yang. Yang is ambition, yang is aggression, yang is desire and projection. Yang is political—yin is religious. Whenever you are ambitious, it is impossible for you to be religious; whenever you are religious, it is impossible for you to be political. The two don't go together. They don't mix. They cannot mix—their very natures are like water and oil. Ambition and meditation can never mix.

THE POLITICIAN FUNCTIONS through the male principle and the sage functions through the feminine principle. That's why the sages become so soft, so feminine, so round, so beautiful. A certain grace surrounds them. And the beauty is certainly not only of the body—sometimes it happens that the body may not be beautiful at all.

In early Christianity, there was a legend that Jesus was the ugliest person in the world. By and by Christians dropped that idea; they didn't like it. But it has something beautiful in it. It said that his body was ugly, yet when you came across Jesus, you would be suddenly surprised, overtaken, possessed, overwhelmed by his beauty. If you had seen a picture of him, you would have seen only his ugliness, but if you had gone to him, entered his actual presence, you would have forgotten all about his ugliness because so much beauty was flowing. So much beauty was pouring out, raining from him, that you would not even remember that he was ugly. So those who had not seen him used to think that he was ugly,

and those who had seen him used to say that he was the most beautiful person of all.

The body is not the question. The sage does not live in the body or as the body, he lives *through* the body. The politician is nothing *but* the body, the extrovert. The body is extrovert, the psyche is introvert, and when you transcend both, Tao arises. When you are neither extrovert nor introvert—when you are not going to the outer nor into the inner, when you are not going anywhere—there is tremendous stillness. There is no movement, because there is no motivation. Your inner flame is no longer wavering because there is no direction to go in, no purpose to fulfill. There is nowhere else to be and nobody else to be; you are absolutely content in the moment. Then you have transcended man and woman and the polarity. In that transcendence is Tao.

This transcendence has been taught in different ways all over the world. Different terms have been used. The explanation of one term will help you to understand. The term is "israel." It is not the name of a certain

> " *If you are dominated by the sun, you will be aggressive, ambitious and political. If you are dominated by the moon, you will be cool, non-aggressive, receptive, peaceful, silent.* "

race—and it is not a name of a certain individual. Israel is exactly what Tao is. Israel is made up of three symbols: *is-ra-el*. *Is* comes from the Egyptian word *isis*. Isis is the Egyptian moon goddess and Ishtar is the Babylonian moon goddess. Thus *is* is the principle of yin, the feminine.

Yoga recognizes three passages in the human being: the moon, the sun, and the transcendental. Through one nostril, you breathe the moon energy; through the other nostril, you breathe the sun energy. Deep inside, when both types of breathing stop, then you transcend.

Ra is the Egyptian sun god. The symbol *Ra* represents the masculine principle, yang. And *El* comes from Elohim, the same root from which the Mohammedans derive "Allah." The Hebrew word for God is Elohim; "el" comes from there. It represents the meeting of the feminine and the masculine and their transcendence—Tao. Israel means Tao exactly.

If you are dominated by the sun, you will be aggressive, ambitious, political—and burning

with desire and passion. If you are dominated by the moon, you will be cool, non-aggressive, receptive, peaceful, silent. But both have to be transcended because both are lopsided. You have to come to the moment when you can say, "I am neither man nor woman." That's when you can become a Buddha or a Christ or a Krishna—when you are neither man nor woman, neither moon nor sun, neither *is* nor *ra*, neither yin nor yang, but simply *is*, purely *is*. All formulations have disappeared.

This transcendence develops only gradually. First you have to drop the principle of *ra*—the principle of the sun, the male energy—and you have to move into the feminine, into the female *is*. And from there you have to move into the beyond. Remember that everything happens through the feminine principle—so whether you are going beyond or you are going below makes no difference— it is the ladder.

With only the body, the sun energy, the male, you will become a rapist. You will rape life; you will not be a lover. Science comes out of sun energy; science is male-oriented. That's why the East has not developed it. The East has lived through the moon principle—passive, silent, easygoing, not trying to conquer—in deep love with nature, not trying to fight. The East has never been a rapist; the West has raped nature. Hence the problems of ecology have arisen: nature is being destroyed.

With the feminine principle, with the moon principle, there is love. You will love. You will not rape. Sometimes the physical act may look the same, but the innermost quality is different.

You can rape even your wife if you don't love her. The physical act of making love to or raping a woman may be similar, but the inner quality differs greatly.

With the sun energy, science is born: it is the rape of nature. With the moon energy, poetry, art, painting, dance, and music are born: it is love playing with nature. The East has lived through art, music, dance, drama. The West has been trying to use male energy too much. The West has lost balance, but so has the East—no society has yet evolved which can be called Israel, which can be called Tao, which has transcended both or synthesized both in such harmony that the antagonism has disappeared.

Tao is the goal: to create a human being who is fully integrated, totally integrated, and to create a human society that is totally integrated as well.

no goal, no technique

All technique is against nature, against Tao. Effort as such is against Tao. If you can leave everything to nature, then no technique is needed, because that is the ultimate technique. If you can leave everything to Tao, that is the deepest surrender possible. You are surrendering yourself, your future, your possibilities. You are surrendering time itself and all effort. This means infinite patience, awaiting.

ONCE YOU surrender everything to nature, there is no effort; you just float. You are in a deep let-go. Things happen to you, but you are not making any effort for them—you are not even seeking them. If they happen, it is okay; if they don't happen, it is okay—you have no choice. Whatsoever happens, happens; you have no expectations and, of course, no frustrations.

Life flows by; you flow in it. You have no goal to reach, because with a goal effort enters. You have nowhere to go, because if you have somewhere to go, effort will come in; it is implied. You have nowhere to go, nowhere to reach, no goal, no ideal, nothing to be achieved —you surrender all. In this surrendering moment, in this very moment, all will happen to you.

Effort will take time; surrender will not take time. Technique will take time; surrender will not take time. That's why I call surrender the ultimate technique. It is a non-technique. You cannot practice it—you cannot practice surrender. If you practice, it is not surrender. Then you are

relying on yourself; then you are not totally helpless; then you are trying to do something— even if it is surrender, you are *trying* to do it. Then technique will come in, and with technique time enters, future enters. Surrender is non-temporal; it is beyond time. If you surrender, this very moment you are out of time, and all that *can* happen will happen. But then you are not searching for it, not seeking it; you are not greedy for it. You have no mind for it at all: whether it happens or not, it is all the same to you.

Tao means surrender—surrender to nature. Then you are not. Tantra and yoga are techniques. Through them you will reach a place of surrender, but it will be a long process. Ultimately after every technique you will have to surrender— but with techniques it will come in the end. With Tao, in Tao, it comes in the beginning. If you can surrender right now, no technique is needed.

You have to be deconditioned. If you are in Tao, then no technique is needed. If you are healthy, then no medicine is needed. Every medicine is against health. But you are ill;

道

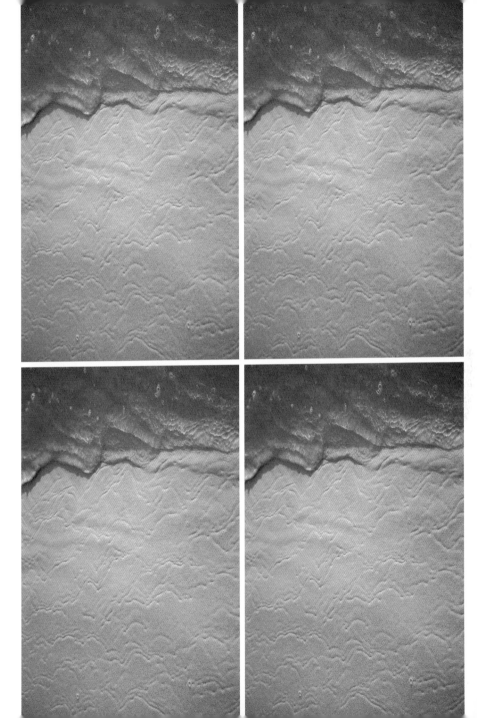

道

medicine is needed. This medicine will kill your illness. It cannot give you health, but if the illness is removed, health will happen to you. No medicine can give you health. Basically every medicine is a poison—but you have gathered some poison; you need an antidote. It will balance, and health will be possible.

Technique is not going to give you your divinity, it is not going to give you your nature. All that you have gathered around your nature it will destroy. It will only decondition you. You are conditioned, and right now you cannot take a jump into surrender. If you can take it, it is good—but you cannot take it. Your conditioning will ask, "How?" Then techniques will be helpful.

When one lives in Tao, then no yoga, no tantra, no religion is needed. One is perfectly healthy; no medicine is needed. Every religion is medicinal. When the world lives in total Tao, religions will disappear. No teacher, no Buddha, no Jesus will be needed, because everyone will be a Buddha or a Jesus. But right now, as you are, you need techniques. Those techniques are antidotes.

You have gathered around yourself such a complex mind that whatsoever is said and given to you, you will complicate it. You will make it more complex, you will make it more difficult. If I say to you, "Surrender," you will ask, "How?" If I say, "Use techniques," you will ask, 'Techniques? Are not techniques against Tao?" If I say, "No technique is needed; simply surrender and godliness will happen to you," you will immediately ask, "How?"—your mind.

If I say, "Tao is right here and now. You need not practice anything, you simply take a jump

and surrender," you will say, "How? How can I surrender?" If I give you a technique to answer you your mind will say, "But is not a method, a technique, a way, against Tao? If divinity is my nature, then how can it be achieved through a technique? If it is already there, then the technique is futile, useless. Why waste time with the technique?" Look at this mind!

Once it happened that a man, the father of a young girl, asked composer Leopold Godowsky to come to his house and give an audition to his daughter. She was learning piano. Godowsky came to their house; patiently he listened to the girl playing. When the girl finished, the father beamed, and he cried in happiness and asked Godowsky, "Isn't she wonderful?"

Godowsky is reported to have said, "She has an amazing technique. I have never heard anyone play such simple pieces with such great difficulty."

This is what is happening in your mind. Even a simple thing you will make complicated and difficult for yourself. This is a defense measure, because when you create difficulty you need not do it—first the problem must be solved, and then you can do it.

Remember, you can go on in this vicious circle continuously forever and ever. You will have to break it somewhere and come out of it. Be decisive, because only with decision is your humanity born. Only with decision do you become human. Be decisive. If you can surrender, surrender. If you cannot surrender, don't create philosophical problems, use some technique. Either way, the surrender will happen to you.

the watercourse way

There are few Taoist temples, so to find a Taoist statue is very rare. Most statues are in the mountains —standing in the open, carved out of the mountain with no roof, no temple, no priest, no worship.

THERE WAS A STATUE of Lao Tzu, the founder of Tao, and a young man had been hoping for years to go to the mountains and see that statue. He loved the words, the way Lao Tzu has spoken, the style of life that he lived, but he had never seen any of his statues. Years passed, and there were always many things preventing the young man from following his desire to see the statue.

Finally one night he decided that he had to go—it was not that far, only a hundred miles. But he was a poor man, and he would have to walk. In the middle of the night—he chose a time in the middle of the night so that his wife and the children and family would be asleep and no trouble would arise—he took a lamp in his hand, because the night was dark, and walked out of the town. As he reached the first milestone outside the town, a thought arose in him: "My God, one hundred miles! And I only have two feet—it is going to kill me. I am asking the impossible. I have never walked one hundred miles, and there is no road."

It was a small footpath into the mountains— dangerous, too. So he thought, "It is better to wait till the morning. At least there will be light and I can see better; otherwise I will fall somewhere, off this small footpath, and without even seeing the statue of Lao Tzu, I will simply be finished! Why commit suicide?" So he stopped and sat down just outside the town.

As the sun was rising, an old man came by. He saw this young man sitting there and he asked, "What are you doing here?" The young man explained. The old man laughed. He said, "Have you not heard the ancient saying? Nobody has the power to take two steps together; you can take only one step at a time. The powerful, the weak, the young, the old— it doesn't matter. The saying goes, 'Just step by step, one step at a time, a man can go ten thousand miles.' And this is only a hundred miles! Who is saying that you have to go continuously? You can take your time; after ten miles you can rest for a day or two days and enjoy. This is one of the most beautiful valleys, among the most beautiful mountains, and the trees are so full of fruits, fruits that you may not have even tasted. Anyway, I am going; you can come along with me.

I have been on this path thousands of times, and I am at least four times your age. Stand up!"

The old man was so authoritative—when he said "Stand up!" the young man simply stood. And the old man said, "Give your things to me. You are young and inexperienced; I will carry your things. You just follow me, and we will take as many rest stops as you want."

What the old man had said was true—as they entered deeper into the forest and the mountains, it became more and more beautiful. There were many wild, juicy fruits to eat and whenever the young man wanted to rest, the old man was ready. He was surprised that the

old man himself never said it was time to rest. But whenever the young man wanted to rest, he was always willing to rest with him— a day or two, and then they would start the journey again.

Those one hundred miles just came and went by, and they reached one of the most beautiful statues of one of the greatest men who has ever walked on the earth. Even his statue was something special—it was not just a piece of art; it was created by Taoist artists to represent the spirit of Tao.

The Tao philosophy is one of letting go. You are not to swim, but to flow with the river, to allow the river to take you wherever it is going, because every river ultimately reaches the ocean. There is no need to be tense or to worry—you will reach the ocean.

In that lonely spot the statue was standing, and there was a waterfall just by its side— because Tao is called the watercourse way. Tao flows just as water goes on and on flowing with no guidebooks, no maps, no rules, no discipline. Strangely enough, it flows in a very humble way, always seeking the lower position everywhere. It never goes uphill. It always goes downhill, and it reaches to the ocean, to its very source. The whole atmosphere surrounding the statue was representative of the Taoist idea of let-go.

The old man said, "Now begins the journey."

The young man said, "What? I was thinking, one hundred miles and the journey is finished."

The old man said, "That is just the way the masters have been talking to people. But the reality is now—from this point a journey of a thousand and one miles begins. And I will not deceive you, because after a thousand and one miles you will meet another old man—perhaps me—who will say, 'This is just a stopover; go on.' Going on is the message."

The journey is endless, but the ecstasy goes on deepening. At each step, you are more; your life is livelier, your intelligence is aflame. And nobody stops. Once the seeker has reached to his being, he himself becomes capable of seeing what lies ahead—treasures upon treasures. Persuasion is needed only up to the point of being; those first one hundred miles are the most difficult. After those one hundred miles, it may be a thousand and one miles or an infinity—it makes no difference.

Now you know that in reality there is no goal; the very talk of the goal was for the beginners, was for children. The journey is the goal.

The journey itself is the goal.

It is infinite. It is eternal.

You will find stars, unknown spaces, unknowable experiences, but you will never come to a point where you can say, "Now I have arrived." Anybody who says, "I have arrived" is not on the path. He has not traveled; his journey has not begun; he is just sitting on the first milestone.

Each departure is a little painful, but the pain will be forgotten immediately—because more and more blissfulness will be showered on you. Soon you will learn this: there is no need to feel pain when you depart from one overnight stay. You become accustomed to

THE WAY

Tao means the way with no goal. Simply, the Way. It was courageous of Lao Tzu, twenty-five centuries ago, to tell people that there is no goal and we are not going anywhere. We are just going to be here, so make the time as beautiful, as loving, as joyous as possible. He called his philosophy Tao, and Tao means simply the Way.

Many asked him, "Why have you chosen the name Tao? Because you don't have any goals in your philosophy."

He said, "Specifically for that reason I have chosen to call it 'the Way,' so that nobody forgets that there is no goal, there is only the Way."

The Way is beautiful; the way is full of flowers. And the Way becomes more and more beautiful as your consciousness becomes higher. The moment you have reached the peak, everything becomes so sweet, so ecstatic, that you suddenly realize that this is the place; this is home. You were unnecessarily running here and there.

So cancel all the tickets you have booked! There is nowhere to go.

leaving because you know that the journey is endless. The treasure becomes greater and greater; you are not losing. Stopping anywhere will be a loss. So there is no stop, no full stop, not even a semicolon....

lao tzu:
"the old guy"

Lao Tzu is just a spokesman of life. If life is absurd, Lao Tzu is absurd; if life has an absurd logic to it, Lao Tzu has the same logic to it. Lao Tzu simply reflects life. He doesn't add anything to it, he doesn't choose out of it; he simply accepts whatsoever it is. It is simple to see the spirituality of Buddha—it is impossible to miss it, he is so extraordinary. But it is difficult to see the spirituality of Lao Tzu. He is so ordinary, just like you. You will have to grow in understanding. Buddha passes by you and you will immediately recognize that a superior human being has passed; he carries the aura of a superior human being around him. It is difficult to miss him, almost impossible to miss him. But Lao Tzu...he may be your neighbor. You may have been overlooking him because he is so ordinary—he is so extraordinarily ordinary, and that is the beauty of it.

道

道

absolute tao

Let me tell you the story of how the verses of Lao Tzu's **Tao Te Ching** *came to be written, because that will help you to understand them. For ninety years Lao Tzu lived—in fact, he did nothing except live. He lived totally. Many times his disciples asked him to write, but he would always say: The Tao that can be told is not the real Tao. The truth that can be told becomes untrue immediately.*

Lao Tzu says: *The Tao that can be told of is not the absolute Tao.*

SO HE WOULD NOT say anything; he would not write anything. Then what were his disciples doing with him? They were only being with him. They lived with him; they moved with him; they simply imbibed his being. Being near him, they tried to be open to him; being near him, they tried not to think about anything; being near him, they became more and more silent. In that silence he would reach them—he would come to them and he would knock at their doors.

For ninety years he refused to write anything or to say anything. His basic attitude was that truth cannot be taught. The moment you say something about truth, it is no longer true—the very saying falsifies it. You cannot teach it. At the most you can indicate it, and that indication should be your very being, your whole life; it cannot be indicated in words. Lao Tzu was against words; he was against language.

It is said that he used to go for a morning walk every day, and a neighbor used to follow

him. Knowing that Lao Tzu was a man of absolute silence, the neighbor also always kept silent. Even a "hello" was not allowed; even talking about the weather was not allowed. To say, "How beautiful a morning!" would be too much chattering. Lao Tzu would walk for miles and the neighbor would follow him.

For years this went on, but once it happened that a guest was staying with the neighbor and he also wanted to come, so the neighbor brought him. The guest did not know Lao Tzu or his ways. He started to feel suffocated because his host was not talking, and he couldn't understand why they were so silent— the silence became heavy on him.

If you don't know how to be silent, silence can become heavy. It is not that by saying things you communicate—no. It is by saying things that you unburden yourself.

In fact, through words, communication is not possible; just the opposite is possible—you can avoid communication. You can create a screen of words around you so that your real situation cannot be known. You clothe yourself with words.

道

That man started feeling naked and suffocated and awkward; it was embarrassing. So he simply said, when the sun was rising, "What a beautiful sun. Look…! What a beautiful sun is born, is rising! What a beautiful morning!"

That's all he said. But nobody responded because the neighbor, his host, knew that Lao Tzu wouldn't like it. And of course Lao Tzu wouldn't say anything at all.

When they came back, Lao Tzu told the neighbor, "Tomorrow, don't bring this man. He is a chatterbox." Yet the guest had only said those few words in a two- or three-hour walk. Lao Tzu said, "He talks uselessly—because I also have eyes, I can see that the sun is being born and it is beautiful. What is the need to say it?"

Lao Tzu lived in silence. He avoided talking about the truth that he had attained and he rejected the idea that he should write it down for the generations to come.

At the age of ninety he took leave of his disciples. He said, "Now I am moving towards the hills, towards the Himalayas. I am going there to get ready to die. It is good to live with people, it is good to be in the world while you are living, but when one is getting nearer to death it is good to move into total aloneness, so that you move toward the original source in your absolute purity and loneliness, uncontaminated by the world."

The disciples felt very sad, but what could they do? They followed him for a few hundred

> " *The truth cannot be said for many reasons. The first and most basic is that truth is always realized in silence.* "

miles, but by and by Lao Tzu persuaded them to go back. He was crossing the border alone and the guard on the border imprisoned him. The guard was also a disciple, and he said, "Unless you write a book, I am not going to allow you to move beyond the border. This much you must do for humanity. Write a book. That is the debt you have to pay, otherwise I won't allow you to cross." So for three days, Lao Tzu was imprisoned by his own disciple.

It was beautiful. It was loving. He was forced—and that's how the small book of Lao Tzu, *Tao Te Ching*, was born. He had to write it, because the disciple wouldn't allow him to cross the border otherwise. Since the guard had the authority and could create trouble for him, Lao Tzu had to write the book. In three days he finished it.

This is the first sentence of the book:
The Tao that can be told of is not the absolute Tao.

This is the first thing Lao Tzu had to say: whatsoever can be said cannot be true. This is the introduction for the book. It simply makes you alert: Now some words will follow, but don't become a victim of the words. Remember the wordless. Remember that which cannot be communicated through language, through words. The Tao can be communicated, but it can only be communicated from being to being. It can be communicated when you are with the master, just with the master doing nothing, not even practicing anything.

Why can't the truth be said? What is the difficulty? The truth cannot be said for many reasons. The first and the most basic reason is that truth is always realized in silence. When your inner talk has stopped, then truth is realized. And that which is realized in silence, how can you express it through sound? It is an experience. It is not a thought.

If it were a thought it could be expressed; there would be no trouble in that. Howsoever complicated or complex a thought may be, a way can be found to express it. The most complex theory of Albert Einstein, the theory of relativity, can also be expressed in a symbol. There is no problem with that. The listener may not be able to understand it; that is not the point. It can be expressed.

It is said that when Einstein was alive, only a dozen persons in the whole world understood him and what he was saying. But even that is enough. If even a single person can understand, it has been expressed. And even if a single person cannot understand right now, maybe after many centuries there will come a person who can understand it. Then too it has been expressed. The very probability that somebody can understand it means that it has been expressed.

But truth cannot be expressed because the reaching of it is through silence, soundlessness, thoughtlessness. You reach it through no-mind; the mind drops. How can you use something that, as a necessary condition, has to drop before truth can be reached? Mind cannot understand truth, mind cannot realize truth, so how can mind express it? Remember it as a rule: If mind can attain something, mind can express it; if mind cannot attain it, mind cannot express it.

All language is futile. Truth cannot be expressed.

Then what have all the scriptures been doing? Then what is Lao Tzu doing? Then what are the Upanishads doing? They all try to say something that cannot be said in the hope that a desire may arise in you to know about it. Truth cannot be said, but in the effort of saying it, a desire can arise in the listener to know that which cannot be expressed.

A thirst can be provoked. The thirst is there; it needs a little provocation. You are already thirsty—how can it be otherwise? You are not blissful, you are not ecstatic—you are thirsty. Your heart is a burning fire. You are seeking something that can quench the thirst but, not finding the water, not finding the source, by and by you have tried to suppress your thirst itself. That is the only way; otherwise, it is too much—it will not allow you to live at all. So you suppress the thirst.

A master like Lao Tzu knows well that truth cannot be said, but the very effort to say it will provoke something, bring the suppressed thirst to the surface. Once the thirst surfaces, a search, an inquiry starts. And he has moved you.

The Tao that can be told of is not the absolute Tao.

At the most it can be relative.

For example, we can say something about light to a blind man, knowing well that it is impossible to communicate anything about light because he has no experience of it. But something can be said about light—theories about light can be created. Even a blind man can become an expert in the theories of light. About the whole science of light he can become an expert—there is no problem in that—but he will not understand what light is. He will understand what light consists of; he will understand the physics of light, the chemistry of light. He will understand the poetry of light, but he will not understand the facticity of it, what light *is*. The *experience* of light he will not understand. So all that is said to a blind man about light is only relative: it is something about light; it is not light itself. Light cannot be communicated.

Something can be said about God, but God cannot be said. Something can be said about love, but love cannot be said. That "something" remains relative. It remains relative to the listener's understanding, intellectual grip, training, and desire to understand. It depends on and it is relative to the master's way of expressing, the devices used to communicate. It remains relative—relative to many things—but it can never become the absolute experience. This is the first reason that truth cannot be expressed.

The second reason that truth cannot be expressed is because it is an experience. No *experience* can be communicated, leave truth aside. If you have never known love, when somebody mentions love, you will hear the word but you will miss the meaning. The word is in the dictionary—even if you don't understand, you can look in the dictionary and know what it means. But the meaning is in you. Meaning comes through experience. If you have loved someone then you know the meaning of the word "love." The literal meaning is in the dictionary, in the language, in the word. But the experiential meaning, the existential meaning, is in *you*. If you have known the experience, immediately the word "love" is no longer empty; it contains something.

If I say anything at all, it is empty unless you bring your experience to it. When your experience comes to it, it becomes significant; otherwise, it remains empty—words and words and words.

How can truth be expressed when you have not experienced it? Even in ordinary life, an unexperienced thing cannot be told. Only words will be conveyed. The container will reach you, but the content will be lost. An empty word will travel toward you; you will hear it, and you will think you understand because you know its literal meaning, but you will miss it. The real, authentic meaning comes through existential experience. You have to know it; there is no other way. There is no shortcut. Truth cannot be transferred. You cannot steal it, you cannot borrow it, you cannot purchase it, you cannot rob it, you cannot beg it—there is no way. Unless you have it, you cannot have it.

The Tao that can be told of is not the absolute Tao.

Remember this condition.

three types of people

Lao Tzu says: When the highest type of people hear the Tao, they try hard to live in accordance with it. When the mediocre type hear the Tao, they seem to be aware and yet unaware of it. When the lowest type hear the Tao, they break into loud laughter—if it were not laughed at, it would not be Tao.

THE GREATEST MYTH is that of humankind. There exists nothing like it. There are as many humankinds as there are people; there is not one kind. Every individual is so different from every other that humanity does not exist. It is just a word, an abstraction. You appear to be similar to others but you are not, and that myth has to be thrown away—only then can you penetrate deeper into the reality of human beings.

No ancient psychology ever believed that humanity existed. In fact, if we are going to classify, then all the ancient psychologies classify man in three divisions. In India, they have divided humanity into three parts: *Satwa*, *Rajas*, and *Tamas*. Lao Tzu has not given these names, but he also divides humanity into three types, exactly the same way.

These three divisions are arbitrary—we have to classify in order to understand; otherwise, there are as many humankinds as there are men and women, every man and woman is a world in himself or herself. But this classification helps to understand many things that would be impossible to understand without it. Try to understand the classification as clearly as possible.

When the highest type of people hear the Tao, they try hard to live in accordance with it. When the mediocre type hear the Tao, they seem to be aware and yet unaware of it. When the lowest type hear the Tao, they break into loud laughter—if it were not laughed at, it would not be Tao.

The first is *Satwa*, the second is *Rajas*, and the third is *Tamas*.

The highest type of person, when he hears about Tao, suddenly feels in tune with it. It is not an intellectual understanding for him: his total being vibrates with a new song; a new music is heard. When he hears the truth, suddenly something fits and he is no longer the same—just hearing, he becomes totally a different type of individual. Not that he has to use his intellect to understand it—that would be a delayed understanding. The highest type of person understands immediately, with no time gap. If he hears a truth, in just the hearing

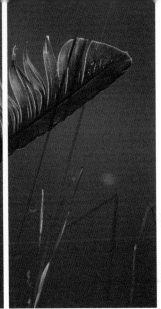

itself, he has understood. His total being understands it, not only the intellectual part. Not only the soul, not only the mind, but even the body vibrates in a new unknown way. A new dance has entered into his being, and now he can never be the same.

Once he has heard the truth he can never be the old way again; a new journey has started. Now nothing else can be done, he has no choice but to move. He has heard about light and he has been living in darkness: now unless he achieves the light, there will be no rest for him. He will become deeply discontented. He has heard that a different type of existence is possible: now unless he attains it, he cannot be at ease, he cannot be at home anywhere. Wherever he is, the constant call from the unknown will be knocking at the door. Waking he will hear it; sleeping he will hear it; dreaming—and the knock will be

there—he will hear it. Eating he will hear it; walking he will hear it; in the market, he will hear it—it will be haunting him all the time.

That's why Krishnamurti always said that there is no need to do anything. In fact, for the first-rate type of person there is no need to do anything—just by hearing, by right listening, one attains. But where to find the first-rate person? They are very rare. Unless a Krishnamurti comes to listen to Krishnamurti, it won't happen. But why should a Krishnamurti go to listen to a Krishnamurti? It is absurd; it has no meaning. A person with that kind of perceptivity can become awakened just by listening to the song of a bird, just by listening to the breeze passing through the trees, just by listening to the sound of water flowing—that's enough, because from everywhere the truth speaks. If you are perceptive, whatsoever you hear you have heard the truth, you have heard

道

the Tao. Nothing else exists. All sounds are divine, all messages are divine, everywhere is the divine signature. For the first-rate mind the path is not a path at all; the person simply enters the temple without any path, there is no need for any bridge.

Lao Tzu says that when the highest type of person hears the Tao there is an immediate perception, an immediate understanding. Just by looking at the master who has attained, just by hearing his word, or just by hearing his breathing, silent, peaceful, sitting by his side, he understands.

Once this type of person understands, then they are not trying to attain truth; they are simply trying to refine their mechanism. They have understood the truth—it exists; they have heard it. Hindus call their scriptures *Shrutis*. The word *shruti* means "that which has been heard." All the scriptures are "that which has been heard."

Once a man of the first-rate intelligence hears truth, he understands it.

Once it happened that a Sufi master suddenly called one of his disciples. Many disciples were sitting in the hall, but he called only one: "Come near to me."

He was standing near the window, and it was a full-moon night. All the disciples watched in wonder. Why had he called the one? Then the old man indicated something outside the window to the young man and said, "Look!" And from that day the young man changed completely.

The others asked, "What happened? There was nothing we know, only the full-moon night. The full moon was there, of course; the night was beautiful, of course; but what has happened to you seems to be completely out of proportion. You are completely transformed. What happened?"

The young man said, "I heard the master, and I was so silent because he called me, I was so without thoughts, so peaceful, that when he indicated the moon something opened inside me: a window. I had a perception that I had never had. I looked at the moon with new eyes; I looked at the moonlight with a new being. Of course, I have seen the view from a faraway state of my mind and I will have to work hard to reach it, but now it exists. Now I know it is a certainty. Now there is no doubt. But I will still have to reach that state because I have looked through the eyes of the master. Those eyes were not mine; he gave his to me; for a single moment, I borrowed them. I have looked through his being. It was not my being, the window was not mine, it was his window, and he allowed me to look through it. But now I know that a different type of existence is possible—is not only possible, is absolutely certain. Now it may take many lives for me to reach that goal, but the goal is certain. No doubt exists in me now, now doubt cannot disturb me—now my journey is clear."

When the highest type of people hear the Tao, they try hard to live in accordance with it.

They hear, they understand, then they try hard to live in accordance with it. They have looked through the window of the master and they have become certain that now it is an absolute fact; it is not a philosophy, not a metaphysics. It is existential. They have felt it, they have known it, but they will have to go a long way before the same perception becomes their own.

They have heard truth, they have understood it, but they will have to move a long way before the truth becomes their being.

The highest type try hard to live in accordance with it—not that by living in accordance with it and trying hard one achieves it, no. Just by trying hard, nobody achieves it—but by trying hard, by and by you come to feel that the effort itself is a barrier in the final stages of the transformation. By trying hard, you come to know that even trying hard is a barrier, and you drop it. Because when you are trying hard to live in accordance with Tao, that life cannot be a spontaneous life, it can be only a forced phenomenon, a discipline, not a freedom. It will become bondage, because all efforts are of the ego. Even the desire to achieve truth comes from the ego. You will drop that, too.

Remember, you can drop effort only when you have made the effort to its utmost. You cannot say, "If that's the case, then I should drop the effort from the very beginning. Why make it?" You will miss the whole point. That's what happened to those who listened to Krishnamurti. He says that no effort is needed. That is right, but it is right only for those who have been making a great effort with their total being. It is true only for *those* people—*they* can drop it.

To become artlessly artful is not possible for those who have not moved through any discipline. Finally an artist has to become completely oblivious of his art; he should forget whatsoever he has learned. But you can forget only that which you have learned. If the art of an artist is effortful, then his art is not perfect.

In Zen they used many methods to teach meditation. They used art also—painting, calligraphy, and other forms. A student would learn painting for ten or twelve years until becoming absolutely technically perfect—not even a single error existed in the technology of the art. Once the artist had become technically perfect, the master would say, "Now you drop it. For two or three years, completely forget it. Throw away your brushes, forget everything you know about painting, and when you have forgotten it completely, then come to me."

Two, three, four, five years, sometimes even more, are needed to forget. It is very difficult. It is difficult first to learn a thing, and more difficult to unlearn it once you have learned it. The second part is essential, fundamental; otherwise, you will be a technician, not an artist.

It is said that a great archer trained his disciple to perfection in archery, and then told him, "Now you forget everything about it." For twenty years the disciple used to come and go to the master, but the master would not say anything, so the disciple had to wait patiently. By and by he completely forgot everything about archery—twenty years is a long time— and he had become almost an old man.

Then one day he came and as he entered the master's room he saw a bow, but he did not recognize what it was. The master came to

him, embraced him, and said, "Now you have become a perfect archer; you have forgotten even the bow. Now go out and look at the flying birds and with just the idea that they should drop, they will."

The archer went out and he couldn't believe it. He looked at the birds flying, almost a dozen birds, and they fell immediately to the ground. The master said, "Now there is no more to do. I was just showing you that when you forget the technique only then will you become perfect. Now the bow and arrow are not needed; they are needed only for amateurs."

A perfect painter does not need the brush and the canvas; a perfect musician does not need the sitar or the violin or the guitar. No, that is for the amateur.

I came across an old musician—he is dead now—who was one hundred and ten years old. He could create music with anything,

anything whatsoever. He would be passing by two rocks and he would create music with them; he would find a piece of iron and he would start playing with it and you would hear beautiful music, such as you have never heard. This was a musician. Even his touch was musical. If he touched you, you would see that he had touched the innermost instrument of your inner harmony and music—suddenly you would start vibrating.

When anything becomes perfect, the effort that was made to learn it has to be forgotten, otherwise the effort remains heavy on the mind. So it is not by trying hard to live in accordance with Tao that the highest type achieve it—no. They try to live in accordance with it, and by and by they start understanding that to live in accordance with nature, no effort is needed. It is like floating in the water: nobody can just float, first you have to learn to

> *A perfect swimmer becomes part of the river; he is a wave in the river. How can the river destroy the wave?*

swim. Don't go to the river or you will be drowned. A person has to learn to swim and when the swimming becomes perfect, he need not swim, he can just be in the river, floating; he can lie in the river as if he is lying in his bed. Now he has learned how to be in accordance with the river; now the river cannot drown him; now he has no more enmity with the river. In fact, he no longer exists separate from the river. A perfect swimmer becomes part of the river; he is a wave in the river. How can the river destroy the wave? When he floats in accordance with the river, he is no longer fighting, resisting, doing something. He is in tune with the river and he can simply float. But don't try this unless you know how to swim; otherwise, you may be drowned.

The same thing happens with Tao. You make a great effort to live in accordance with the truth, and by and by you understand that your great effort helps a little, but hinders a lot. To live in accordance is to let go, it is not to fight with nature. To live in accordance with nature is to be one with nature; there is no need to struggle. Effort is struggle; effort means that you are trying to do something according to you.

Science is effort; Tao is effortlessness. Science is violence to nature. That's why scientists continually talk in terms of conflict and conquering. It is a fight, as if nature is your enemy and you have to dominate it. Science has a deep political relationship with nature, a deep war, an enmity. Tao is not a fight at all; in fact, it is understanding that you are part of nature. How can the part fight with the whole? And if the part tries to fight with the whole and then becomes anxiety-ridden, what can you expect? It is natural. If the part tries to fight with the whole, if my hand tries to fight with my whole body, the hand will become ill. How can the hand fight with the body? The body supplies the blood, the body supplies the nourishment, how can it fight with the body? The hand fighting with the body is foolish.

Man fighting with nature is foolish. We can live only in accordance with nature. Tao is surrender; science is a war. Science strengthens the ego and the whole problem is how to drop the ego. Through effort it cannot be dropped.

So remember this:

When the highest type of people hear the Tao, they try hard to live in accordance with it.

That is their first standpoint. Once they understand, they hear, they feel, they taste the affinity with it, and they start the hard effort to live accordingly. But as they grow in it, they begin to understand that effort is not needed—rather, effortlessness. Finally they drop effort and become one with nature.

Somebody asked Lao Tzu, "How did you attain?"

A LEAF FALLS AND SETTLES

If history is to be written rightly then there should be two kinds of histories: the history of doers—Genghis Khan, Tamerlane, Nadirshah, Alexander, Napoleon Bonaparte, Ivan the Terrible, Joseph Stalin, Adolf Hitler, Benito Mussolini; these are the people who belong to the world of doing. There should be another history, a higher history, a real history—of human consciousness, of human evolution: the history of Lao Tzu, Chuang Tzu, Lieh Tzu, Gautam Buddha, Mahavira, Bodhidharma; totally different kind of history.

Lao Tzu became enlightened sitting under a tree. A leaf had just started falling—it was in the autumn, and the leaf was zig-zagging with the wind, slowly. He watched the leaf. The leaf came down to the ground, settled on the ground, and as he watched the leaf falling and settling, something settled in him.

From that moment, he became a non-doer. The winds come on their own, and existence takes care.

Lao Tzu was the contemporary of the great thinker, moralist, and law giver, Confucius.

Confucius belongs to the other history, the history of the doers. Confucius had great influence over China—and has influence even today.

Chuang Tzu and Lieh Tzu were the disciples of Lao Tzu. These three people have reached to the highest peaks, but nobody seems to be impressed by them. People are impressed when you do something great. Who is impressed by somebody who has achieved a state of non-doing?

道

He said, "I was sitting under a tree and I had done all that could be done, all that was humanly possible, and I was completely frustrated. Much had happened through it, but not all; something was lacking, missing, and the missing link was the most difficult to find, elusive. Then while I was sitting under a tree, a leaf, a dry leaf, fell from the tree slowly, and moved in the wind. The wind was going north, the leaf moved north; then the wind changed course, started moving toward the south, and the leaf started moving toward the south, then the wind stopped—and the leaf fell down on the earth, with not a single complaint, with no struggle, with no direction of its own. If the wind was going south, it was going south; if the wind was going north, it was going north; if the wind stopped, it fell down on the earth and rested beautifully.

"Then again there was some wind and again it rose high in the sky—but there was no problem. Suddenly I understood. The message hit home. From that day I became a dry leaf and the missing link that had been so elusive was elusive no more." The missing link was only this: you can attain many things through effort, but you cannot attain Tao through effort. Finally you have to leave effort—and suddenly everything fits, you are in accordance. Then you don't give direction, then you are no longer a director; you don't say to the winds: Go south, because I am on a journey toward the south. You have no destination; the destiny of the whole is your destiny; you are not separate. You no longer think in terms of individuality; you have become part of the whole and wherever the whole is going you are going. If the whole changes its mind, you change your mind; if the whole stops the journey, it is beautiful; if the whole runs, you run with it. That is what "in accordance" means.

With not a bit of mind of your own, when you have become a no-mind, the whole lives through you, lives you, moves through you, moves you. Now you don't breathe, the whole breathes you. Everything is a benediction, a blessing. How can you be tense then? Worried about what? All worries exist because you have brought an individual destiny into your mind against the destiny of the whole—you are moving upstream.

This is the secret of your failure—you are moving upstream. You are worried, tense, in anguish, in anxiety, almost going mad—anybody will go mad if they are constantly going upstream because the fight is so hard and so meaningless. One day you will feel tired and then it will look like a frustration, a failure. The wise man leaves this upstream nonsense; he simply allows the river to take him wherever it is going. If it is going anywhere, good; if it is not going anywhere, good.

Suddenly you are still, silent. Only then, never before, does real meditation happen and all effort is dropped. But you have to make the effort first, otherwise you will never understand that it has to be dropped.

When the mediocre type hear the Tao they seem to be aware and yet unaware of it.

That's what the mediocre mind is—a little bit aware. A little understanding and a little

non-understanding, a little part lighted and a little part in darkness, divided. To be divided is to be mediocre. To be divided against yourself is to be mediocre because it dissipates your energy; it can never allow you to be overflowing, celebrating existence. If you are trying to create a fight between your right and left hand, how can you be happy? The fight itself will kill you and there will be no result from it, because how can the left win, or how can the right win? Both hands are yours.

Any type of inner conflict makes you mediocre, and those who teach you to be divided are your enemies. They say, "This is bad and that is good." Immediately division enters. They say, "This is lower, that is higher."

Immediately division enters. They say, "This is sin and that is virtue." Immediately division enters. You are split. The whole of humanity is schizophrenic and everybody has become mediocre.

To be one is to be blissful; to be divided is to be in misery. To be one is to be in heaven; to be divided is to be in hell. The more divided, the greater will be the hell—and you will be a crowd—not only two, but many. Psychologists say that humans have become polypsychic: a person has not one mind now, he has many minds. In small matters also you have many minds—whether to eat this or to eat that, whether to order this or that? It is as if you have lost all possibility of being decisive, because you can only be decisive if you are one, a unit.

How can you be decisive? When one voice says this, another voice immediately contradicts and says that; one voice says

go east; another says go west. If you are pulled against yourself in so many directions, your whole life will be a sad failure, a long tale of frustration and nothing else—"a tale told by an idiot, full of sound and fury, signifying nothing."

Significance is possible only when there is unity within. The highest type of people can attain unity, the lowest type also have a certain type of unity, but the mediocre ones are in the greatest danger.

You can see wise persons like Buddha or Lao Tzu in unity—bliss surrounds them, they move surrounded by a subtle ecstasy, and if you look at them you can see they are drunk with the divine. They walk on the earth but they are not here. But you can sometimes also feel the same type of vibe around an idiot. A certain innocence surrounds him—he laughs, and you can glimpse the sage in the idiot because he is also one. He is not a sage, he has not attained anything, but at least he is not divided.

A sage has gone beyond the mind while an idiot is below the mind. In this one thing they are equal: neither of them have any mind. There are vast differences, but there is also this one similarity. If you don't understand, a sage can sometimes look like an idiot—and sometimes, in your ignorance, you can worship an idiot for a sage. I have come across many idiots being worshipped—they have a certain quality; at least they are one. They don't have much mind—in fact, they don't have a mind at all, they have no thoughts.

BE USELESS

Lao Tzu was wandering with his disciples and they came to a forest where hundreds of carpenters were cutting trees, because a great palace was being built. The whole forest had been almost cut, but only one tree was standing there, a big tree with thousands of branches—so big that ten thousand persons could sit under its shade. Lao Tzu asked his disciples to go and inquire why this tree had not been cut yet when the whole forest had been cut and was deserted.

The disciples went and asked the carpenters, "Why have you not cut this tree?"

The carpenters said, "This tree is absolutely useless. You cannot make anything out of it because every branch has so many knots in it. Nothing is straight. You cannot make pillars out of it. You cannot make furniture out of it. You cannot use it as fuel because the smoke is so dangerous to the eyes—you might go blind. This tree is absolutely useless. That's why."

They came back. Lao Tzu laughed and he said, "Be like this tree. If you want to survive in this world be like this tree—absolutely useless. Then nobody will harm you. If you are straight, you will be cut, you will become furniture in somebody's house. If you are beautiful, you will be sold in the market, you will become a commodity. Be like this tree, absolutely useless. Then nobody can harm you. And you will grow big and vast, and thousands of people can find shade under you."

> *I can give you the flower, but how can I give you the fragrance? You have to cleanse your nose and become more sensitive.*

I lived in a town for many years, and near that town lived a saint who was famous, and people used to come from all over India to see him. He was a perfect idiot, but he had a certain beauty around him—no anxiety, no problems. A few problems might have existed for him, but because people started worshipping him, even those problems were not there. People would bring food and everything else for him so even the problem of basic survival was not there. They even made a beautiful house for him.

Yet if you watched him, you could see that he didn't understand a thing. I went to see the man many times and I watched him closely. He was absolutely mentally damaged—he could not utter a single word—but people thought that he had taken a vow of silence for his whole life. There was no glimmer in his eyes of any alertness, but still there was a similarity. People have been deceived many times. Of course, these poor people can't deceive you; it is your own gullibility. You are deceived by your own self. Many times it has happened that very rare souls have been thought to be idiotic, because there is a similarity to what happens with the idiot.

The idiot is one part, the superhuman being is one part, and then there is the middle part, the mediocre, which is the majority in the world.

"The mediocre part," says Lao Tzu, "... seems to be aware and yet unaware of it." When you talk about truth, the mediocre mind understands it intellectually but does not understand it totally. That person says, "Yes, I can understand what you are saying but still I miss something. What do you mean?" The word is heard, but the meaning is lost. The mediocre person can understand intellectually—he may be educated, he may be a graduate, even have a PhD. He understands what you are saying because he understands language, but something is being lost. He understands the word, but the word is not the message. The message is subtle; it can come with the word, but it is not the word.

The word is like a flower and the meaning is like the fragrance that surrounds it. If your nose is not functioning well, I can give you a flower but I cannot give you the fragrance. If your mind is not functioning totally, I can give you a word but I cannot give you the meaning. The meaning has to be detected by you, decoded by you. I can give you the flower, but how can I give you the fragrance? If your nose is not functioning, if your nose is insensitive, then nothing can be done—I can give you a thousand and one flowers, but you will not smell the fragrance.

Many people come to me and say, "Whatsoever you say, we understand, but nothing happens. We have understood

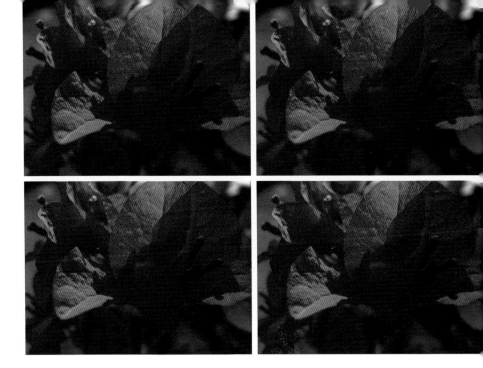

everything you have said, we have read your books many, many times, we have underlined almost every line—but nothing is happening."

I can give you the flower, but how can I give you the fragrance? You have to cleanse your nose and become more sensitive. That is where meditation can be helpful: it makes you more sensitive, more alert. It pushes you toward the first type, and by and by you start feeling—not only understanding, but feeling. Feeling is needed. I don't mean that you should become sentimental. Sentimentality is not feeling; sentimentality is a false coin. There are people who can weep and cry for nothing and they think they are the feeling type. They are not. They are only sentimental.

Feeling is a mature quality; sentimentality is an immature quality. A person of feeling will do something; a person of sentimentality will create more trouble. For example, if somebody is ill or dying, the person of feeling will go to the hospital and try to help the one who is dying. The man or woman of sentimentality will start crying and weeping. They will create more trouble for the dying person—they will not even allow the person to die in silence. Sentimentality is chaos; feeling is substantial growth. When I talk about love, if you have feeling, then not only your head understands, but also your heart starts throbbing in a different way. The fragrance has reached you.

Meditation can help you by throwing out all the dust and dirt that you have collected within you, all that is stopping your sensitivity.

The doors of your perception are covered with dirt. You would like to see rightly, but there are so many suppressed tears that they won't allow a clear eye. You would like to smell the flower, but you cannot, because the whole of civilization has been suppressing your nose. You may not be aware that the nose is the most suppressed part of the body. Humans have lost the sense of smell almost completely.

Horses and dogs are more sensitive than humans. What is happening to your nose? Why has it gone dead? There is a subtle mechanism working here because smell is deeply concerned and connected with sex. Have you seen animals smelling each other before they make love? They will never make love unless they smell first, because through scent they feel if their body energies will meet or not, whether they are meant for each other or not. Smelling is a kind of antenna. A dog moves, smells: if the female dog suits his sense of feeling and sense of smell, only

then does he make the effort; otherwise, they move on their separate ways. He is not worried at all. That female dog is not for him; he is not for her.

Smell is the most sexual sense in the body and when civilization decided to suppress sex, automatically civilization decided to suppress smell also. Whenever a woman wants to make love, she suddenly starts emitting subtle scents around herself and that would be dangerous in a world where sex is not accepted. If you walk on the street with your wife and, looking at some other man, she starts emitting the scent, you will know it immediately! Then your wife cannot deceive you; she cannot say that she had not even looked at that man. But as it is now, the wife herself cannot know that her body is throwing off a certain scent, neither can the man to whom she has become suddenly attracted. Your noses are completely closed; you don't smell. And in that way things are beautifully settled, no trouble arises.

So if you really want to smell the flower— if you want not only to carry the flower but to enjoy the scent as well—then you will have to come to a more natural state of non-repressed sexuality. Otherwise it will not be possible. If all your five senses are covered with dust and dirt and suppressed, they will create a mediocre mind, because the mind is nothing but a collective reservoir of all the five senses. When you are mediocre, then you can go on becoming more and more scholarly, but you will remain a fool because you will not be alive.

Have you watched the phenomenon that pundits are the most dead people you can ever see? Professors and scholars are the most dead people. They don't see, they don't smell, they don't taste—they are almost dead since all their senses are dead. Only their head functions, alone, without any support from the body. If you cut off their body they would not be worried, only don't disturb their head. They will, on the contrary, be very happy if the head can function without the body. Then they can go on and on in their scholarly trips with no trouble from the body. No illness will disturb them; no hunger will disturb them.

A scholar does not know even his hunger. He lives in the head. Scholars are always mediocres, perfect mediocres, and the problem for the mediocre is that he understands—that deceives him, because he thinks that he understands, it is finished. Yet he doesn't understand a bit; he remains unaware. His understanding is only of the head, not of the total being. And unless understanding is of the total being, it is not understanding at all. Intellectual understanding is not understanding at all; that is a misnomer.

When the lowest type hear the Tao, they break into loud laughter.

The lowest type think this truth, this Tao, is some sort of joke. They are so shallow that nothing about the depth appeals to them and the laughter is a protection. The shallow people laugh because now you are being funny. They know well that there is no truth at all, that nothing like truth exists; it is just an invention of cunning people to exploit other people. The loud laughter is a protection because they are also afraid, afraid that the thing may exist. Through laughter they brush it away, they throw it away. Through laughter they show derision, condemnation, the belief that the whole thing is nonsense. At the most you can laugh at it and nothing else. You will come across the lowest type everywhere. If a lowest type sees a Lao Tzu he will laugh: "This man has gone mad; one more man is lost to humanity and has gone mad."

If the lowest man sees you meditating, he will laugh, he will think that you seem to be a little eccentric. What are you doing? Why are you wasting your time? If he can laugh ,he can feel very good about himself that he is not as mad or as foolish as this meditating person is.

Says Lao Tzu:

If it were not laughed at, it would not be Tao.

Lao Tzu says, *If the third type does not laugh when it hears about truth, it will not be truth.* So this is a definite indication: whenever truth is asserted the lowest type will immediately laugh. It shows two things certainly: one, that truth has been asserted, and second, that a third, a lowest person, has heard about it. Between truth and the lowest person, laughter happens; between the mediocre person and the truth an intellectual type of understanding happens; between the first type of person and truth a deep understanding of total being happens—the person's total being throbs with an unknown adventure, a door has opened into a new world.

LAO TZU AND CONFUCIUS

It is said that Confucius went to see Lao Tzu. Lao Tzu was an old man and Confucius was younger. Lao Tzu was almost unknown and Confucius was almost universally known. Kings and emperors used to call Confucius to their courts; wise men used to come for his advice; he was the wisest man in China in those days. But by and by he must have felt that although his wisdom might be of use to others, he was not blissful; he had not attained anything. He had become an expert, maybe helpful to others, but not helpful to himself.

So he started a secret search to find someone who could help him. Ordinary wise men wouldn't do, because they came to him for his advice. Great scholars wouldn't do; they came to ask him about their problems. But there must be someone somewhere—life is vast. He sent his disciples to find someone who could be of help to him, and they came back with the information that there lived a man—nobody knew his name—known as "the old guy."

Lao Tzu means "the old guy." It is not his name; nobody knows his name. He was such an unknown man that nobody knows when he was born or to whom, nor who his father was or who his mother was. He lived for ninety years but only rare human beings had come across him who had different eyes and perspectives from which to understand him. He was only for the rarest—so ordinary a man, but only for the rarest of human minds.

Hearing the news that a man known as "the old guy" existed, Confucius went to see him. When he met Lao Tzu, he could feel that here was a man of great understanding, great intellectual integrity, great logical acumen—a genius. He could feel that something was there, but he couldn't catch hold of it. Vaguely, mysteriously, there was something; this man was no ordinary man, although he looked absolutely ordinary. Something was hidden; he was carrying a treasure.

Confucius asked, "What do you say about morality? What do you say about how to cultivate good character?"—because he was a moralist and he thought that if you cultivated a good character that was the highest attainment.

Lao Tzu laughed loudly and said, "If you are immoral, only then does the question of morality arise. If you don't have any character, only then do you think about character. A man of character is absolutely oblivious of the fact that anything like character exists. A man of morality does not know what the word *moral* means. So don't be foolish! And don't try to cultivate. Just be natural."

The man had such tremendous energy that Confucius started trembling. He couldn't withstand him and so he escaped. He became afraid, as one becomes afraid near an abyss. When he came back to his disciples, who were waiting outside under a tree, the disciples could not believe it. This man

had been going to emperors, the greatest emperors, and they had never seen any nervousness in him. Now he was trembling, and cold sweat was pouring from all over his body. They couldn't believe it—what had happened? What had this man Lao Tzu done to their teacher? They asked him, and he said, "Wait a little. Let me collect myself. This man is dangerous."

About Lao Tzu, he said to his disciples, "I have heard about great animals like elephants, and I know how they walk. I have heard about animals hidden in the sea, and

I know how they swim. And I have heard about great birds who fly thousands of miles across the earth, and I know how they fly. But this man is a dragon. Nobody knows how he walks. Nobody knows how he lives. Nobody knows how he flies. Never go near him—he is like an abyss. He is like a death."

And that is the definition of a master: a master is like death. If you come near him, too close, you will feel afraid; trembling will take over. You will be possessed by an unknown fear, as if you are going to die. It is said that Confucius never went again to see this old man.

chuang tzu:
natural and ordinary

Chuang Tzu was one of the most natural men the world has seen. He has not given any discipline, he has not given any doctrine, he has not given any catechism. He has simply explained one thing: that if you can be natural and ordinary, just like the birds and the trees, you will blossom, you will have your wings open in the vast sky.

道

道

easy is right

Chuang Tzu says:

Easy is right. Begin right and you are easy.
Continue easy, and you are right.
The right way to go easy is to forget the right way
and forget that the going is easy.

EASY IS RIGHT. Nobody has dared to say it, ever. On the contrary, people make the "right" as difficult as possible. To everyone that has been conditioned by different traditions, the wrong is easy and the right is arduous. It needs training, it needs discipline, it needs repression, it needs renouncing the world, it needs renouncing pleasures....

Lies are easy, truth is difficult—that is the common conditioning of humanity.

But Chuang Tzu is certainly a man of tremendous insight. He says, *Easy is right.*

Then why have people been making the right difficult? All the saints have been making the right difficult. There is a psychology behind it: only the difficult is attractive to your ego. The more difficult the task, the more the ego feels challenged.

Climbing Everest was difficult; hundreds of people died in the attempt before Edmund Hillary reached the top alive. For a whole century, groups upon groups of mountaineers had been making the effort. And when Edmund Hillary reached the top, there was nothing to be found! At the very peak there is only space enough for one person to stand there, on the highest point. He was asked, "What prompted you? Knowing perfectly well that dozens of mountaineers have lost their lives over the years, and not even their bodies have been found... why did you try this dangerous project?"

He said, "I had to try. It was hurting my ego. I am a mountaineer, I love climbing mountains, and it was humiliating that Everest existed and nobody had been able to reach there. It

> *A state of awareness is just like a cat: even when she is asleep she is alert.*

is not a question of finding anything... I feel immensely happy."

What is this happiness? You have not found anything! The happiness is that your ego has become more crystallized. You are the first man in the whole of history who has reached the peak of Everest; now nobody can take your place. Anybody else who reaches there will be second, third...but you have made your mark on history; you are the first. You have not found anything but a deep nourishment for your ego.

All the religions make the right difficult, because the difficult is attractive—attractive to the ego. But the ego is not the truth; the ego is not right. Do you see the dilemma? The ego is attracted only to the difficult. If you want people to become saints you have to make your right, your truth, your discipline very difficult. The more difficult it is, the more egoists will be attracted, almost magnetically pulled.

But the ego is not right. It is the worst thing that can happen to a person. It cannot deliver to you the right, the truth; it can only make your ego stronger. Chuang Tzu is saying in a simple statement, the most pregnant statement: *Easy is right.* Because for the easy, the ego has no attraction. If you are moving toward the easy, the ego starts dying. When there is no ego left, you have arrived at your reality—at the right, at the truth.

Truth and right have to be natural. Easy means natural; you can find the real and the true without any effort. "Easy is right" means *natural* is right, *effortlessness* is right, *egolessness* is right.

Begin right and you are easy; continue easy and you are right.

They are just two sides of the same coin. If, beginning to live a right life, you find it difficult, then remember: it is not right. If, living the right, your life becomes more and more easy, more and more a let-go, a flowing with the stream, then it is right.

Going against the stream is difficult, but going with the stream is not difficult. So either choose the easiest things in life, the most natural things in life, and you will be right; or if you want to begin the other way, remember the criterion that the right has to produce easiness and relaxation in you.

Continue easy and you are right. Never forget for a moment that the difficult is food for the ego, and the ego is the barrier that makes you blind, makes you deaf, makes your heart hard to open, and makes it impossible for you to love, to dance, to sing.

Continue easy. Your whole life should be an easy phenomenon. Then you will not be creating the ego. You will be a natural being. The ordinary is the most extraordinary. The people who are trying to be extraordinary

have missed the point. Just be ordinary; just be nobody.

All your conditionings corrupt you. They say, To be easy is to be lazy, to be ordinary is humiliating. If you don't try for power, for prestige, for respectability, then your life is meaningless—that idea has been forced into your mind.

Chuang Tzu in his simple statements is taking away all your conditionings. *Continue easy and you are right.* Never for a moment get attracted to the difficult. It will make you "somebody"—a prime minister, a president— but it will not make you divine. Easy is divine.

I have heard about a wealthy American man. He had been striving all his life to be on the top and he had reached it, and had all the things the world can offer. But he felt stupid inside, because there was nothing on the top.

If Edmund Hillary was intelligent enough, he must have felt stupid standing on Everest. Why had he been striving so hard? The man who walked on the moon must have felt a little embarrassed, although there was nobody who could see his face. This man had come to the top as far as money was concerned, and as far as money could purchase, he had purchased everything. Now he was feeling stupid.

"What is the point of it all?" Inside he felt hollow. He had no time to give to his inner growth, no time even to be acquainted with himself.

He dropped all his riches and rushed to the East to find the truth, because three-quarters of his life was almost gone—just the tail end remained; the elephant had passed by. But if

NO WAY

It is said that the first time Chuang Tzu entered the hut where Lao Tzu, his would-be master, was living, Lao Tzu looked at him and said, "Remember one thing: never ask me how to become enlightened." The poor fellow had come for that very purpose. But Lao Tzu made it clear: "Only on this condition will I accept you as my disciple."

There was a moment of silence. Chuang Tzu thought, "It is strange. I have come to become enlightened; that is the very purpose of becoming a disciple. And this old fellow is asking such an absurd thing: if you want to be my disciple, promise me that you will never ask about how to become enlightened."

But it was already too late. He had fallen in love with the old man. He touched his feet and he said, "I promise I will never ask how to become enlightened, but accept me as your disciple."

Immediately came a hard slap, "You idiot! If you are not going to become enlightened, then for what purpose are you becoming a disciple? I was asking this promise because I could see in you such beautiful intelligence that you might have immediately realized the point of my asking. You are enlightened; there is no way to become enlightened. There is no need. In fact even if you want to become unenlightened, there is no way."

道

something might be possible, then there were a few days left. He rushed from one master to another, but nobody could satisfy him because whatever they said was another trip for the ego, and he was well acquainted with that trip.

It does not matter whether you are accumulating money or whether you are accumulating virtue, whether you are becoming respectable here or you are becoming respectable hereafter—it does not matter, it is the same game. Whether you are becoming a world-famous celebrity or a world-worshipped saint, there is no difference: both are ego trips.

All these gurus were trying to give him difficult disciplines and arduous ways of finding the truth; they were all saying, "It may not be possible in this life, but start anyhow. In the next life maybe.... The journey is long, the goal is a faraway star."

But now nobody could deceive him. He had understood that just "becoming somebody special" is an exercise in stupidity.

Finally he heard about a saint who lived in the Himalayas. The people said, "If you are not satisfied with him, you will never be satisfied with anybody. Then forget the whole thing."

So, tired and tattered, after walking for miles, finally he found the old man. He was happy upon seeing the old man, but he was shocked. Before he could say anything, the old man asked, "Are you an American?"

He said, "Yes, I am."

The old man said, "Very good. Have you got any American cigarettes with you?"

He said, "My God, where am I? I have come to seek truth, to find the right..." He pulled out

his cigarettes and the old man took one and started smoking.

The American said, "You have not even asked me why I have come here, tired, hungry..."

The old man said, "That does not matter."

The American said, "I have come to find the truth!'

The old man said, "Truth? You do one thing—go back where you came from. And next time when you come, bring a lot of American cigarettes, because here in this place it is difficult to find cigarettes. I am an easygoing man. I don't make any effort; people come on their own. But I like the best cigarettes."

"But," the man asked, "...what about my search?"

The old man said, "Your search? This is the discipline for you: go back, buy as many cigarettes as you can, and come back and remain here with me."

The man asked, "Any discipline?"

The old man said, "I am an ordinary old man—no discipline, no religion, no philosophy—I only like to smoke cigarettes. You come here, and slowly, slowly you will also become just as ordinary as I am. And I tell you, to be ordinary, with no pretensions, is the right."

And as the man turned to go back, puzzled, the old man said, "Listen, at least leave your wristwatch here, because I don't have any wristwatch so I never know the time. And anyway, you are going back, so you can buy yourself another wristwatch."

Chuang Tzu would have liked this old man. *Easy is right. Begin right and you are*

easy. That has to be the criterion. If you feel uneasiness, tension, then what you have started cannot be right.

Continue easy and you are right.

And the last part is something never to be forgotten. *The right way to go easy is to forget the right way*—because even to remember it is an uneasiness. *The right way to go easy is to forget the right way and forget that the going is easy.* What is the need of remembering these things?

Relax to such a point... be as natural as the trees and the birds. You will not find in the birds that somebody is a saint and somebody is a sinner; you will not find in the trees that somebody is virtuous and somebody is full of vices. Everything is easy—so easy that you need not remember it.

Chuang Tzu was one of the most natural men the world has seen. He has not given any discipline, he has not given any doctrine, he has not given any catechism. He has simply explained one thing: that if you can be natural and ordinary, just like the birds and the trees, you will blossom, you will have your wings open in the vast sky.

You don't have to be a saint. Saints are tense—more tense than sinners. I have known both, and if there is a choice I will choose the sinners as a company rather than the saints. Saints are the worst company, because their eyes are full of judgment about everything: "You should do this and you should not do that." And they start dominating you, condemning you, humiliating you, insulting you, because what they are doing is the right, and what you are doing is not

the right thing. They have poisoned your nature so badly that if real criminals are to be found, they will be found in your saints, not in your sinners. Your sinners have not done much harm to anybody.

I have visited jails, met criminals, and I was surprised that they are often the most innocent people. Perhaps because they are the most innocent they have been caught—the cunning ones are doing far greater crimes, but they are not caught. Every law has loopholes. The cunning ones find the loopholes first; the innocent ones get caught because they don't have that cunningness.

It is a strange world in which we are living. The criminals are the rulers, the criminals are politicians, the criminals become presidents, vice presidents, prime ministers—because, except for a criminal, who wants power? An authentic human being wants peace, love, to be left alone, and the freedom to be himself. The very idea of dominating others is criminal.

Chuang Tzu is right: if you feel any tension, whatever you are doing is not right. And he is the only man who has given such a beautiful criterion:

Easy is right.

Begin right and you are easy.

Continue easy, and you are right.

The right way to go easy is to forget the right way and forget that the going is easy.

Relax into nobodiness. Be natural. Become part of this relaxed universe—so relaxed that you forget all about easiness and you forget all about rightness.

THE HAPPY TURTLE

Two messengers came from the Emperor. Chuang Tzu was fishing, and they came to him and said, "The Emperor wants you to become the prime minister of the country."

Chuang Tzu said, "Do you see that turtle there, wagging its tail in the mud?"

They said, "Yes, we see."

"And do you see how happy he is?"

They said, "Certainly. He looks tremendously happy."

And then Chuang Tzu said, "I have heard that in the king's palace there is a turtle, three thousand years old, dead, encaged in gold, decorated with diamonds, and he is worshipped. If you ask this turtle who is wagging his tail in the mud to change his role, to become that turtle in the palace—dead, but encaged in gold, decorated with diamonds, and worshipped by the emperor himself—will this turtle be ready to accept that?"

The messengers said, "Certainly not. This turtle will not be ready."

So Chuang Tzu said, "Why should I be ready? Then be gone! I am happy in my mud, wagging my tail, and I don't want to come to the emperor's palace."

道

the value of that which is useless

Life is dialectical, and that is why it is not logical. Logic means that the opposite is really opposite, and life always implies the opposite in itself. In life, the opposite is not really the opposite, it is the complementary. Without it nothing is possible. For example, life exists because of death. If there is no death, there cannot be any life. Death is not the end and death is not the enemy—on the contrary, because of death, life becomes possible. So death is not somewhere in the end, it is involved here and now. Each moment has its life and its death; otherwise, existence is impossible.

Hui Tzu said to Chuang Tzu:

"All your teaching is centered on what has no use."

Chuang Tzu replied:

"If you have no appreciation for what has no use, you cannot begin to talk about what can be used. The earth, for example, is broad and vast, but of all this expanse a man uses only a few inches upon which he happens to be standing at the time.

"Now suppose you suddenly take away all that he is not actually using, so that all around his feet a gulf yawns, and he stands in the void with nowhere solid except under each foot, how long will he be able to use what he is using?"

Hui Tzu said: "It would cease to serve any purpose."

Chuang Tzu concluded: "This shows the absolute necessity of what is supposed to have no use."

THERE IS LIGHT; there is darkness. For logic they are opposites and logic will say: If it is light, there cannot be any darkness; if it is dark, then there cannot be any light. But life says quite the contrary. Life says, If there is darkness it is because of light; if there is light, it is because of darkness. We may not be able to see the other when it is hidden just around the corner.

There is silence because of sound. If there is no sound at all, can you be silent? How can you be silent? The opposite is needed as a background. Those who follow logic always go wrong because their life becomes lopsided. They think of light, then they start denying darkness; they think of life, then they start fighting death.

One tradition says that God is light, and another tradition says that God is darkness.

Both are wrong, because both are logical: they deny the opposite. And life is so vast, it carries the opposite in itself. The opposite is not denied, it is embraced.

Once somebody said to Walt Whitman, one of the greatest poets ever born, "Whitman, you are contradicting yourself. One day you say one thing, another day you say just the opposite."

Walt Whitman laughed and said, "I am vast. I contain all the contradictions."

Only small minds are consistent, and the narrower the mind, the more consistent. When the mind is vast, everything is involved: light is there, darkness is there, God is there, and the devil too, in his total glory.

If you understand this mysterious process of life, which moves through the opposites, which is dialectical—where the opposite helps, gives balance, gives tone, makes the background— then only can you understand Chuang Tzu— because the whole Taoist vision is based on the complementariness of the opposites.

The two words, yin and yang, are opposites: male and female. Just think of a world that is totally male or a world that is totally female—it will be dead.

The moment it is born, it will be dead; there cannot be any life in it. If it is a female world— women, women, and women, and no men— the women will commit suicide!

The opposite is needed because the opposite is attractive. The opposite becomes the magnet to pull you; the opposite brings you out of yourself; the opposite breaks your prison; the opposite makes you vast.

> ❝ *Whenever the opposite is denied there will be trouble. And that is what we have been doing, hence so much trouble in the world.* ❞

Whenever the opposite is denied there will be trouble. And that is what we have been doing, hence so much trouble in the world.

Man has tried to create a society which is basically male, that is why there is so much trouble—the woman has been denied: she has been thrown out. In past centuries the woman was never to be seen anywhere. She was hidden in the back chambers of the house, not even allowed in the drawing room. You couldn't meet her on the streets, you couldn't see her in the shops. She was not part of life. The world went ugly, because how can you deny the opposite? The world became lopsided; all balance was lost. The world went mad.

In many cultures the woman is still not allowed to move in life; she is really not yet a part, a vital part of life. Men move in male-oriented groups—the exclusive men's club where boys meet, the market, politics, the scientific group. Everywhere it is lopsided. The man dominates, that is why there is so much misery. And when one of the polar opposites dominates, there will be misery because the other feels hurt and takes revenge. So every woman takes her revenge in the house. When she cannot go out and move in the world and take revenge on humanity, on mankind, she takes revenge on her husband. There is constant conflict.

Why is the wife always in conflict? It is not the person; it is not a personal thing. It is the revenge of the woman, of the female, of the denied opposite. And this man in the house, the husband, is the representative of the whole male world, the male-oriented world that she is fighting.

By negating the opposites you invite trouble—and on every path, on every level, in every dimension, it is the same thing.

Chuang Tzu says that if you deny the useless, then there will be no use in the world. If you deny the useless, the playful, the fun, there cannot be any work, any duty. This is difficult because our whole emphasis is on the useful.

If somebody asks you what a house consists of, you will say the walls. And Chuang Tzu would say, just like his master Lao Tzu, that a house consists not of walls but of doors and windows. Their emphasis is on the other part. They say that walls are useful, but their use depends on the useless space behind the walls. A room is space, not walls. Of course, the space is free and the walls have to be purchased. When you purchase a house, what do you purchase? The walls, the material, the visible. But can you live in the material? Can you live in the walls? You have to live in the room, in the vacant space.

So really, what is a house? Emptiness surrounded by walls. And what is a door? There is nothing—"door" means there is nothing, no wall, just emptiness. But you

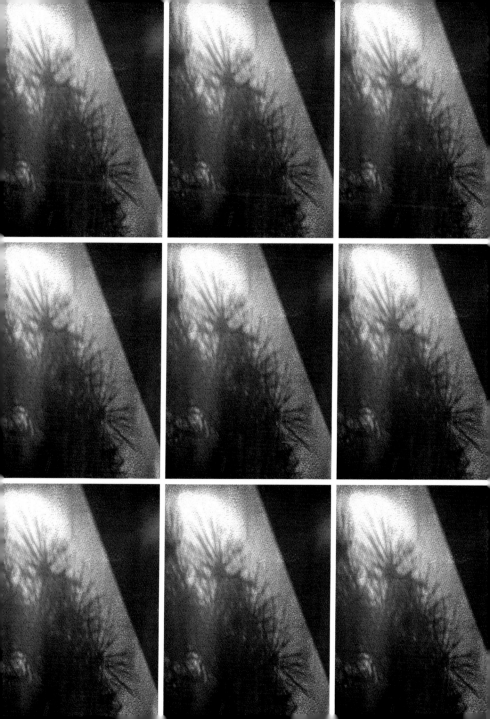

cannot enter the house if there is no door; if there is no window, then no sun will enter, no breeze will blow. You will be dead and your house will become a tomb.

Chuang Tzu says: Remember that the house consists of two things: the walls, the material—the marketable, the utilitarian—and the emptiness surrounded by the walls, the non-utilitarian, which cannot be purchased, which cannot be sold, which has no economic value. How can you sell emptiness? But you have to live in the emptiness—if a man tries to live only in the walls he will go mad; it is impossible to do. But we try to do the impossible. In life, we have chosen the utilitarian.

For example, if a child is playing and you say, "Stop! What are you doing? This is useless. Do something useful. Learn, read, at least do your homework, something useful. Don't wander around, don't be a vagabond." If you continue insisting on this to a child, by and by you will kill the useless—then the child will have become just useful, and when a person is simply useful, he is dead. You can use him, he is a mechanical thing now—a means, not an end unto himself.

You are truly yourself when you are doing something useless—painting, but not to sell, just to enjoy; gardening, just to enjoy; lying down on the beach, not to do anything, just to enjoy. Useless fun, sitting silently next to a friend.

Much could be done in these moments. You could go to the shop or the market; you could earn some money. You could change time into money. You could add to your bank balance, because these moments will not come back and foolish people say that time is money. They know only one use for time: to convert it into more and more money. In the end you die with a big bank balance, but inside you are totally poor, because the inner richness arises only when you can enjoy the useless.

What is meditation? People ask, "What is the use of it? What will we gain out of it? What is the benefit of it?" Meditation...and you ask about the benefit? You cannot understand it because meditation is useless. The moment I say "useless," you feel uncomfortable because the whole mind has become so utilitarian, so commodity-oriented, that you always ask for a result. You cannot concede that something can be a pleasure unto itself.

Useless means you enjoy it but there is no benefit from it; you are deeply merged in it and it gives you bliss. But when you are deeply in it, you cannot accumulate that bliss, you cannot make a treasury out of it.

In the world, two types of people have existed: the utilitarians, who become scientists, engineers, doctors; and the other branch, the complementary type, of poets and vagabonds—useless, not doing anything useful. But they provide the balance, they give grace to the world. Think of a world full of scientists and not a single poet—it would be absolutely ugly, not worth living in. Think of a world with everyone working in the shops and offices: not a single vagabond. It would be hell. The vagabond gives beauty.

Two vagabonds were arrested. The judge asked the first one, "Where do you live?"

The man said, "The whole world is my home, the sky is my shelter; I go everywhere, and there is no barrier. I am a free man."

Then the judge asked the other, "And where do you live?"

The second vagabond said, "Next door to him."

These people give beauty to the world, they bring a perfume. A Buddha is a vagabond; a Mahavira is a vagabond. This man, this vagabond, answered that the sky was his only shelter. That is what is meant by the word *digamber*. Mahavira, the last great master of the Jains, is known as "*digamber*." *Digamber* means naked, with only the sky for clothing, nothing else. The sky is the shelter, the home.

When the world becomes too utilitarian, you create many things, you possess many things, you become obsessed with things—but the inner is lost, because the inner can flower only when there are no outer tensions, when you are not going anywhere, when you are just resting. Then the inner flowers. The greatest has always happened when you are not doing anything. Only the trivial happens when you are doing something.

Soren Kierkegaard, the Danish philosopher, has written something very penetrating. He said, "When I started praying, I would go to the church and talk to God...." That is what Christians are doing all over the world. They talk to God in a loud voice, as if God is dead. And as if God is just a foolish entity, they advise him what to do and what not to do. Or, as if God is just a foolish monarch, they persuade him or bribe him to fulfill the desires that are in them.

But Kierkegaard said, "I started talking, then suddenly I realized that this was useless. How can you talk to God? One has to be silent. What is there to be said? And what can I say that will help God to know more? He is omnipotent, he is omniscient, he knows all, so what is the purpose of my telling him?"

And Kierkegaard said, "I talked to him for many years, then suddenly I realized that this was foolish. So I stopped talking, I became silent. Then after many years I realized that even silence wouldn't do. Then the third step was taken, and that was listening. First I was talking, then I was not talking, and then I was listening."

Listening is different from just being silent, because just being silent is a negative thing—listening is a positive thing. Just being silent is passive, while listening is an alert passiveness: waiting for something, not saying anything, but waiting with the whole being. Listening has an intensity. And Kierkegaard said, "When this listening happened, then for the first time prayer happened."

But it seems listening is absolutely useless, especially listening to the unknown; you don't know where it is. Silence is useless, talking seems to be useful. Something can be done through talking; by talking you do many things in the world. So you think that if you want to become religious you will also have to do something.

But Chuang Tzu said: Religion begins only when you have understood the futility of all doing, and you have moved to the polar opposite of nondoing, inactivity, of becoming passive, becoming useless.

THE DONKEY'S SHADOW

It is said about Chuang Tzu that one evening he was talking to his disciples and many of them were fast asleep, as disciples are. It must have been late at night and they were tired, and Chuang Tzu was saying difficult things that were beyond them. When something is beyond you, it seems better to rest and sleep than to bother with it.

Suddenly Chuang Tzu became aware that many of the disciples were fast asleep and it was useless. Some were even snoring and disturbing him. So he told a parable. He said: "Once it happened that a man had a donkey and he was traveling on a pilgrimage to some holy place. But he was very poor, and it came to pass that he was hungry. No money was left, so he sold the donkey on which he was riding to another traveler, who was rich. But the next afternoon, when the sun was very hot, the first owner rested in the shadow by the side of the donkey.

"The second owner said, 'This is not good. You have sold the donkey to me.'

"The first owner said, 'I have sold the donkey, but not the shadow.'"

Everybody became alert—suddenly nobody was asleep, nobody was snoring. When you talk about donkeys, donkeys hear it immediately! Chuang Tzu said, "Now I come back to my point...."

But all the disciples said, "Wait! Please finish the story." Now everybody was throbbing with excitement: "What happened? Then what happened?"

Chuang Tzu said, "It was a parable, not a story. You are more interested in donkeys than you are in me." Chuang Tzu left the story there, he never completed it. It was not meant to be completed, it was just an indication that the human mind is more interested in stupidities than in higher values; it is more interested in foolish things.

Chuang Tzu and his master Lao Tzu were always talking about the useless; they even praised men who were useless.

Chuang Tzu talks about a man, a hunchback. All the young people of the town were forcibly entered into the military, because they were useful. Only this one man, the hunchback, who was useless, was left behind. Chuang Tzu said: Be like the hunchback, so useless that you are not slaughtered in the war.

They praise the useless because they say that the useful will always be in difficulty. The world will use you; everybody is ready to use you, manipulate you, and control you. If you are useless nobody will look at you; people will forget about you. They will leave you in silence; they will not bother about you. They will simply become unaware that you exist.

It happened to me. I am a useless man. In my childhood days I would be sitting down

next to my mother. She would look around her and say, "I would like to send someone to fetch vegetables from the market, but there is no one to send"—and I would be sitting there right next to her! She would say, "I don't see anyone around," and I would laugh inside myself—she couldn't send me to the market—I was so useless that she was not aware that I was there.

Once my aunt came to stay, and she was not aware of my uselessness. My mother was saying, "Nobody is available to go to the market. All the children have gone out and the servant is ill, so what can I do? Some one has to be sent."

My aunt said, "Why not send Raja? He is sitting there, not doing anything."

So I was sent. I asked the market vendor there, "Give me the best vegetables you have got, the best bananas, the best mangoes." Looking at me and hearing the way I was talking, he must have thought I was a fool, because nobody ever asks for the best. So he charged me double and gave me all the rotten things he had, and I came home very happy.

My mother threw them away and said, "Look! This is why I say nobody is here."

Chuang Tzu insists: Be alert and don't be very useful; otherwise, people will exploit you. Then they will start managing you and then you will be in trouble. And if you can produce things, they will force you to produce all your life. If you can do a certain thing, if you are skillful, then you cannot be wasted.

He says that uselessness has its own intrinsic utility. If you can be useful for others, then you have to live for others. Useless, nobody looks at you, nobody pays any attention to you; nobody is bothered by your being. You are left alone. In the marketplace you can live as if you are living in the Himalayas. In that solitude you grow. Your whole energy can move inward.

Chuang Tzu says, "If you have no appreciation for what has no use, you cannot begin to talk about what can be used." The useless is the other aspect of the useful. You can talk about the useful only because of the useless. It is a vital part. If you drop it completely, then *nothing* will be useful. Things are useful because there are things that are useless.

But this is what has happened to so many people in the world. We cut out all playful activities, thinking that then the whole of our energy will move into work. But now work has become a bore.

You have to move to the opposite pole—only then will you be rejuvenated. The whole day you are awake and at night you fall asleep. What is the use of sleep? It is wasting time—and not just a little time. If you live to ninety years of age, for thirty years of your life you will be asleep, eight hours every day, one third of each day. What is the use of it?

But at the end of the whole day's work, when you fall asleep you move from the useful to the useless. And that is why in the morning you feel so fresh, so alive, so unburdened. Your legs have a dancing quality, your mind can sing, your heart can again feel—all the dust of work is thrown off, the mirror is again clear.

You have clarity in the morning. How does it come? It comes through the useless.

That is why meditation can give you the greatest glimpses, because it is the most useless thing in the world. You don't do anything—you simply move into silence. It is greater than sleep, because in sleep you are unconscious and whatever happens, happens unconsciously. You may be in paradise, but you don't know it. In meditation you move knowingly. You become aware of the path: how to move from the useful world of the outer to the useless world within. Once you know the path, at any moment you can move inward. Sitting in a bus, you do not need to do anything; traveling in a car or train or an airplane, you are not doing anything. Everything is being done by someone else; you can close your eyes and move into the useless, the inner. Suddenly everything becomes silent, and suddenly everything becomes cool, and suddenly you are at the source of all life.

Meditation has no value on the market. You cannot sell it, you cannot say, "I have great meditation. Is anybody ready to buy it?" Nobody will buy it. It is not a commodity; it is useless.

Chuang Tzu says:

"If you have no appreciation for what has no use, you cannot begin to talk about what can be used. The earth, for example, is broad and vast, but of all this expanse a man uses only a few inches upon which he happens to be standing at the time. Now suppose you suddenly take away all that he is not actually using, so that all around his feet a gulf yawns, and he stands in the void with nowhere solid except under each foot, how long will he be able to use what he is using?"

This is a beautiful metaphor. You are sitting in a chair, and you are using only a small space, two by two. You are not using the whole earth; the rest of the earth is useless. Says Chuang Tzu, Suppose the whole earth is taken away, only two by two is left for you? Suppose you are standing with each foot using a only few inches of earth—suppose only that is left, and the rest of the earth is taken away—how long will you be able to use this small part that you are using?

A gulf, an infinite abyss, yawns around you—you will get dizzy immediately and you will fall into the abyss. The useless earth supports the useful—and while the useless is vast, the useful is very small. This is true on all levels of being: the useless is vast and the useful is very small. If you try to save only the useful and forget the useless, sooner or later you will get dizzy. And this has already happened, you are already dizzy and falling into the abyss.

All over the world, thinking people have a problem: life seems to be meaningless. Ask Sartre, Marcel, Jaspers, Heidegger—they say life is meaningless. Why has life become so meaningless? It never used to be so. Buddha never said it; Krishna could dance, sing, enjoy himself; Mohammed could pray and thank God for the blessing of life. Chuang Tzu is happy, as happy as a person can possibly be. These people never said that life was meaningless.

What has happened to the modern mind? Why does life seem so meaningless?

The whole earth has been taken away and you are left only the part on which you are sitting or standing. You are getting dizzy. All around you, you see the abyss and the danger. You cannot use the earth on which you are standing now, because you can use it only when the useless is joined with it. The useless has to be there.

What does it mean? Your life has become only work and no play. The play is the useless, the vast; the work is the useful, the trivial, the small. You have filled your life completely with work. Whenever you start doing something, the first thing that comes to the mind is, what is the use of it? If there is some use, you do it.

Sartre sets one of his stories in the twenty-first century. A very rich man says, "Love is not for me, it is only for poor people. As far as I am concerned my servants can do it."

Of course, why should a Henry Ford waste time making love to a woman? A cheap servant can do that; Ford's time is more valuable. He should put it to some greater use.

It is possible! Looking at the human mind as it is, it is possible that in the future only servants will make love. When you can send a servant, why bother yourself? When everything is thought of in terms of economics, when a Ford or a Rockefeller can make so much better use of their time, why should they waste their time with a woman? They can send a servant; that will be less trouble.

It looks absurd, but it has already happened in many dimensions of life. You

> *Life seems meaningless because the meaning arises in a balance between the useful and the useless.*

are not an active participant in fun; others do it for you. You go to see a football match: others are playing and you are just watching. You are a passive spectator, not involved. You go to a movie and watch others making love, creating war, violence, everything while you are just a spectator in the seat. It is so useless you need not bother to do it. Anyone else can do it, you can just watch. Work *you* do—fun, others do for you.

Life seems meaningless because the meaning arises in a balance between the useful and the useless. You have denied the useless completely. You have closed the door. Now only the useful is there, and you are burdened too much by it. It is a sign of success that by the age of forty you have ulcers. If you are now fifty and still the ulcers have not appeared, you must be a failure. What have you been doing all your life? You must have been wasting time. By fifty you really ought to have had your first heart attack. And by sixty the really successful man is gone—and he never lived. There was no time to live. He had so many more important things to do, there was no time to live.

Look all around you, look at successful people—politicians, rich men, big industrialists—what is happening to them? Don't look at the things they possess, look at them directly, because if you look at the things you will be deceived. Things don't have ulcers, cars don't have heart attacks, and houses are not hospitalized. Look at the person bereft of all his possessions; look directly at him, and then you will feel his poverty. Then even a beggar may be a rich man; then even a poor man may be richer as far as life is concerned.

Success fails, and nothing fails like success, because the person who succeeds is losing his grip on life—on everything. The person who succeeds is really bargaining, throwing away the real for the unreal, throwing away inner diamonds for colored pebbles on the shore; collecting the pebbles and losing the diamonds. But because you look with the eyes of ambition, you look at the possessions. You never look at the politician; you look at the post, the prime ministership. You look at the power. You never look at the person who is sitting there absolutely powerless, missing everything, not even having a glimpse of what bliss is. He has purchased power, but in purchasing it he has lost himself. The inner self is being lost for futile possessions. You can deceive others, but how will you be able to deceive yourself? In the end you will look at your life and you will see that you have missed it because of the useful.

The useless must be there. The useful is like a garden: neat, clean. The useless is like a vast forest: it cannot be so neat and clean. Nature has its own beauty and when everything is neat and clean, it is already dead. A garden cannot be alive, because you prune it, cut it, manage it. A vast forest has vitality, a powerful soul. Go into a forest and you will feel the impact; get lost in a forest and you will see the power of it. In a garden you cannot feel the power; it is not there, because the garden is man-made. It is beautiful, but it is cultivated, managed, and manipulated.

A garden is a false thing—the real thing is the forest. The useless is like a vast forest and the useful is like a garden you have created around your house. Don't cut into the forest. Let your garden be a part of the vast forest that is not your garden, but nature's garden.

Chuang Tzu emphasized uselessness so much because you have emphasized the useful too much. That emphasis is needed just to give you balance. You have gone too much to the left; you have to be pulled to the right.

But remember, because of this overemphasis you can easily move to the other extreme. And that happened to many followers of Chuang Tzu. They became addicted to the useless and missed the point. Chuang Tzu emphasized the useless only because you have become so addicted to usefulness. But I must remind you—because mind can move to the opposite and remain the same—that the real thing is transcendence. You have to come to a point where you can use the useful and the non-useful, the purposeful and the purposeless. When you are beyond both, they both serve you.

道

A real, a perfect man, a man of Tao, has no addictions. He can move easily from one extreme to another because he remains in the middle. He uses both wings.

Chuang Tzu should not be misunderstood, that is why I say this. People like Chuang Tzu are dangerous because you can misunderstand them, and there is more possibility for misunderstanding than understanding. The mind says, "Okay, enough of this shop, enough of this family...now I will become a vagabond." That is misunderstanding. You will carry the same mind, you will become addicted to being a vagabond. Then you will not be able to come back to the shop, to the market, to the family. Then you will be afraid of it.

In the same way, medicine can become a new disease if you get addicted to it. So the doctor has to see that you get rid of the disease but don't become addicted to the medicine; otherwise, he is not a good doctor.

First you have to get rid of the disease, and immediately afterward you have to get rid of the medicine; otherwise, the medicine will take the place of the disease and you will cling to it always.

Mulla Nasruddin was teaching his small son, who was seven years old, how to approach a girl, how to ask her to dance, what to say and what not to say, how to persuade her. The boy went away and half an hour later came back and said, "Now teach me how to get rid of her!" That has to be learned too, and that is the difficult part. To invite is very easy, but to get rid of is difficult. You know it well through your own experience. Remember, the useless has its own attraction. If you are very troubled by the useful, you may move to the other extreme too much. You may lose your balance. What is needed is a deep balance, standing in the middle, free from all the opposites. You can use the useful and you can use the non-useful; you can use the purposeful and the non-purposeful and still remain beyond both. You are not used by them. You have become the master.

THE RASCAL SAINT

Few people had the courage to remain with Chuang Tzu. He was always creating embarrassing situations; saints were not supposed to do such things. For example, he was seen one day in the capital riding on a donkey with his disciples following him. The whole town was laughing—people were gathered on both sides of the road—because he was not sitting in the right way. The donkey was going forward, and Chuang Tzu was sitting backward on the donkey, facing his disciples!

The townspeople were laughing and the disciples were very embarrassed. Finally one disciple said, "Why are you doing this? You are making a fool of yourself, and along with you we are being ridiculed unnecessarily. People think we are idiots!"

Chuang Tzu said, "There is something great implied in it—I have thought it over. If I sit the way people normally sit on donkeys, then my back will be facing you, and that is insulting.
I don't want to insult anybody, not even my own disciples.

"The other possibility is that you could walk in front of me, but then you will be insulting me—and that is not right either, the disciples insulting the master. So this is the solution that I have found.

"Let the fools laugh—but I am facing you and you are facing me. That's how a master and disciple should be: I am respectful toward you, and you are respectful toward me.

"And the donkey has no objection—why should we bother about what some people think?"

Now this kind of man is rare, unique, difficult to find. He attained to the highest clarity, consciousness, love, compassion—but he remained a rascal to the very end.

道

lieh tzu:

a master storyteller

Lieh Tzu is one of the most perfect expressions of the inexpressible. Truth cannot be expressed: that inexpressibility is intrinsic to truth. Thousands and thousands of people have tried to express it—very few have succeeded even in giving a reflection of it. Lieh Tzu is one of those few; he is rare.

道

道

expressing the inexpressible

Lieh Tzu's approach is that of an artist—the poet, the storyteller—and he is a master storyteller. His experience has flowered into parables; that seems to be the easiest way to hint at that which cannot be said. A parable is a great device; it is not just an ordinary story. Its purpose is not to entertain you; its purpose is to say something that there is no other way to say.

LIFE CANNOT BE put into a theory: it is so vast, infinite. A theory by its very nature is closed. A theory has to be closed; if it is a theory it cannot be open-ended, otherwise, it will be meaningless. A parable is open-ended: it says something and yet leaves much to be said—it only hints. That which cannot be said can be shown. A parable is a finger pointing to the moon. Don't cling to the finger—it is irrelevant—look at the moon. Parables in themselves are beautiful, but their purpose is not in clinging to them—they go beyond; they are transcendental. If you dissect the parable you will not come to much understanding.

It is like the navel in the body—if you ask a surgeon what the purpose of the navel is and he dissects the body, he will not find any purpose. The navel seems to be useless.

What is the purpose of the navel? It was purposeful when the child was in the womb; its purpose was to connect the child to the mother. But now that the child is no longer in the womb—the mother may have died, the child has grown old—now what is the purpose of the navel? The navel has a transcendental purpose; the purpose is not in itself. You will have to look everywhere to find what it indicates. It indicates that the person was once a child, that the child was once in the womb of a mother, that the child was connected to the mother. The navel is just a mark left on the body by the past.

Just as the navel shows something about the past, a parable shows something about the future. It shows that there is a possibility of growing, of being connected with existence. Right now that is only a possibility; it is not actual. If you just dissect the parable, it becomes an ordinary story. If you don't dissect it but drink the meaning of it, the poetry of it, the music of it—forget the story and just look for the significance of it—soon you will see that it indicates a future, indicates something that can be, but is not yet. It is transcendental.

So the first thing to understand about Lieh Tzu is that he is not a theoretician. He will

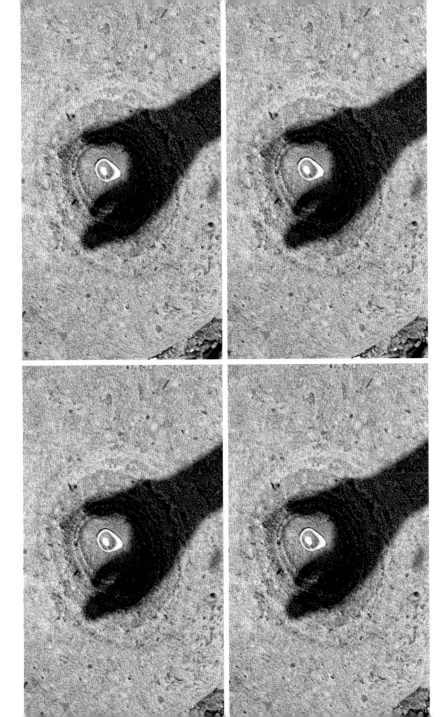

not give you any theories; he will simply give you parables.

A theory can be dissected—its meaning is in it, it has no transcendence, the meaning is immanent. A parable cannot be dissected—dissect it, and it will die. The meaning is transcendental. You have to live a parable, then you will come to its meaning. It has to become your heart, your breathing; it has to become your inner rhythm.

To understand a man like Lieh Tzu, you will have to live an authentic life. Only then, through your own experience, will you be able to feel what he means by his parables. It is not that you can learn the theories and become informed; the information will not help. Unless you know, nothing is going to help. If these parables create a thirst in you to know, a great desire to know, a great hunger to know; if these parables lead you on an unknown journey, on a pilgrimage—only then, by treading the path, will you become acquainted with the path.

Western scholars have been puzzled about Lieh Tzu—about whether he ever existed or not. There are great treatises about him; they worked hard for years to find out whether this man really existed. To the Eastern mind this whole scholarship looks stupid because it does not matter whether he existed or not. If you ask me whether he existed or not, I say it is all the same. Whoever wrote these beautiful stories was Lieh Tzu—whoever the person was, one thing is certain: *somebody* wrote them. That much is certain because these stories exist.

Now, whether somebody by the name of Lieh Tzu really wrote the stories that are attributed to him or somebody by some other name wrote them, how does it make any difference? It will not add anything to the stories; they are already perfect. It will not take anything away from the stories; nothing can be taken away. Whether Lieh Tzu was an historical person or not, how is that going to affect the stories? The stories are beautiful; they have intrinsic value. One thing is certain, somebody wrote them—why be bothered about the writer's name, whether it was Lieh Tzu or something else?

It is possible that they were written by many people—then too there is no problem. Whoever wrote any one of these stories must have touched the consciousness of Tao; otherwise, they could not have been written. One person or many people may have written them, but whenever these stories were written, somebody had penetrated the consciousness of Tao; somebody had understood what life is, somebody had a vision.

In the West this question of authorship is felt to be significant. People have written books and books about whether Shakespeare ever existed or not—as if it makes any difference! The plays that Shakespeare wrote are so beautiful—why not look into the plays and love and enjoy them? It seems to be going astray to ask whether Shakespeare existed or not. And the problem arises because it is thought that Shakespeare was an uneducated man, so how could he write such beautiful things?

Have you ever known very educated men to write beautiful things? It is thought by some that it was not Shakespeare but Lord Bacon

who was the real author. But I cannot trust this because I have read Lord Bacon's other books—they have nothing to compare with Shakespeare. Lord Bacon is just ordinary. He may have been a very learned man, he may have been a great scholar, but his books are ordinary rubbish. Just because he is Lord Bacon and has a famous name, who is deceived? Have you ever heard the name of any book by Lord Bacon? How could Lord Bacon write these Shakespearian plays? Under his name he has not written a single masterpiece, so how could he write one under a pseudonym? And if he could write such beautiful plays as the Shakespearian plays are, under a pseudonym, then what was he doing when he was writing under his own name? It doesn't seem right.

So whether Shakespeare was known as Shakespeare or not is not the point. Some consciousness certainly existed that gave birth to these beautiful plays. What is wrong with calling that consciousness Shakespeare?

In the East, we have never bothered about these things. We say, "What does it matter who wrote something?" If the books are beautiful, very beautiful, tremendously significant, and if we have enjoyed them down the centuries and we have loved them and contemplated them, the authorship is irrelevant.

Whether or not Lieh Tzu really existed is uncertain. He does not seem to be an historical person at all because he has not left any trace. Either he was not an historical person or he was a great horse. My preference is for the second—he was a great horse who never

raised any dust and who never left any tracks behind. He effaced himself completely. Only one small book exists—the *Book of Lieh Tzu* —with a few small parables.

This book says nothing about Lieh Tzu. But why should we bother? Lieh Tzu may have been a woman; he may not have been a man. Who knows? He may not have been Chinese; he may have been Tibetan. Who knows? He may not have *been* at all. It does not matter. But the parables matter. These parables are doors. So please don't chase after the non-essential. Look into the spirit of the essential. Don't be bothered by the gross; go into the subtle.

the nature of knowing

One of the most fundamental questions that has always faced humanity, and that will always encounter every human being ever born, is the nature of knowledge. What is real knowing? Only through knowing does one attain liberation, only through knowing does one come to know oneself, only through knowing is the truth revealed.

MAN IS BORN IN IGNORANCE. The darkness is tremendous. Naturally, the first question that any intelligent being will ask is how to find light. What is light? We are born in darkness not knowing who we are. What greater darkness can there be? We are not even aware of who we are, from where we come, or to where we are going. We are groping somehow, drifting somehow. We are accidental. We don't yet have a destiny. We are unconscious. We have not yet attained to the light of inner being that can enlighten our path. In this darkness, if failure happens, it is natural. In this darkness, if frustration happens, what more can you expect? In this darkness, if you only die and never live, it seems logical.

The fundamental question is: What is the nature of knowledge? What is real knowledge? We know many things and yet remain ignorant. We know many things but the fundamental thing is missing. It is as if we have made a big building and the foundation is missing.

HITTING THE TARGET

Lieh Tzu was studying archery and he hit the target. He sought advice from Kuan-Yin who asked him, "Do you know why you hit the target?"

"No."

"It won't do yet."

Lieh Tzu went away to practice and after three years again reported to Kuan-Yin.

"Do you know why you hit the target?"

"I know."

"It will do. Hold onto this awareness and do not lose it."

This applies not only to archery, but also to ruling oneself. Therefore the sage scrutinizes not the fact of survival or ruin, but its reasons.

Humanity knows much—the knowledge has grown every day—and yet deep down we remain as ignorant as ever. We must have misunderstood the very nature of knowledge.

Before we enter this symbolic and very significant parable, a few things have to be understood.

First, unless you know yourself, all knowing is useless. Unless you know yourself, all knowing is only pseudo-knowing—you appear to know but you don't really know; it is a deception. You know science, you know *things*, you know the world—but you don't know yourself. If the knower himself is in deep darkness, all his knowledge is superficial. It cannot even be skin deep. Scratch the surface of knowledge and soon you will find ignorance coming out. Just scratch a little and knowledge will not be of any help. You will find each person as ordinary and ignorant as any other.

If you insult Albert Einstein, he becomes as angry as anybody else. If Albert Einstein fails,

he feels as frustrated as anybody else. If Bertrand Russell succeeds he is as happy as anybody else. There is no basic difference, because the innermost core remains the same. Bertrand Russell, of course, knows more than you, but the knowledge is quantitative. He is not more of a *knower* than you; the knowledge is not yet *qualitative*. As far as your being is concerned, he is the same as you. He has more information but not more knowing. More information is not more knowing—and more knowing does not necessarily mean more information.

Buddha may not know as much as Bertrand Russell knows—but Buddha is a knower and Bertrand Russell is not. Buddha's knowledge is not about things; his knowledge is about his own being. His knowledge is not an accumulation of information; his knowledge is an explosion, an inner explosion of light.

That's why we call it enlightenment.

He has become more aware—that is his knowing. He no longer walks unalert and inattentive. If you hit him, he will not react the way an unconscious man will react. He will *respond*, but he will not *react* at all. And his response will not be because you have insulted him; his response will be out of his awareness. His response will not be mechanical—that's why I say it will not be a reaction.

A reaction is a mechanical thing; anybody can push your buttons and you react mechanically. You don't have any control over your own mechanism. If somebody insults you, you are insulted. The other person is the master: he pushed a button and you fell under his control. If somebody appreciates you, you are flowing and happy; if he pushes another button, you are under his control.

You can praise Buddha or you can condemn Buddha, but it will not make any difference. You can try to push the buttons, but Buddha will not react. He is not a machine anymore.

Once Buddha was insulted. He was passing through a village and many people gathered and insulted and condemned him. Their anger was almost righteous, because Buddha was destroying the very foundation of their rotten culture. He was destroying the laws that Manu had prescribed for the Hindus. He was destroying the foundation of this class-divided society—a society divided into castes, *varna*. And he was destroying the foundation of the ancient sannyas, because in the ancient days a sannyasin meant a very old man. After seventy-five years of age, you had to become a sannyasin—when life had already ebbed, you were supposed to become a sannyasin, renounce everything, and take up the spiritual life. But Buddha was initiating young people, even young children.

He was destroying two basic fundamentals of Hindu society. The first was *ashrama*, the four stages of life—sannyas is the fourth stage, the last. And the second was the four-caste system, *varna*. In this system the Brahmin is the highest caste and the Sudra is the lowest, and in between is the Vaishya and the Kshatriya. Buddha was destroying this system because he said that anyone who knows Brahma is a Brahmin—not by birth, but by knowing, by being. He said that everybody is born as a Sudra, as an untouchable, the lowest—Brahmins included. At birth, nobody is higher and nobody is lower; at birth everybody is born

as an animal. Then if you work, grow, seek and search, and refine your consciousness, by and by, slowly, you move higher—from the Sudra you become a Vaishya.

A Vaishya is a businessman. He is a little higher, has a few more values in life, thinks sometimes about music, sometimes about poetry. The Sudra is one who thinks only of the body—he eats, sleeps, and that is all. Eat, drink, and be merry—that is his whole circle of life. If you are doing only that you are a Sudra, the lowest category of human being.

Everybody is born that way. You cannot expect a small child to be interested in music, poetry, philosophy and religion. When a child is born he is a hedonist, an Epicurean. He sleeps for eighteen to twenty hours—what more can you expect? Whenever he feels hungry he awakes and cries and weeps—and finds food and nourishment. Then again he falls asleep. He eats, drinks, and sleeps. Every child is a Sudra.

As you start growing, new dimensions open in your being. You start becoming interested in things that are not only of the body. A little of the mind, a little of psychology enters into your being. You are no longer just a physique. Then you are a Vaishya. Then you are moving in the bigger business of life: you are a businessman. Not a very high state, but better than the Sudra.

Then comes the Kshatriya, the warrior. He becomes a little more interested in higher things. He starts searching for truth, for beauty, for love. His interest is higher than the businessman's. And he is ready to

> *As you start growing, new dimensions open in your being.*

stake his life, he is ready to lose his life, for these higher values. He is ready to gamble; he is courageous. Courage enters him. The businessman is not courageous; if everything goes well, he may enjoy music, he may enjoy poetry, he may sit in his home, centered and secure—and think about the truth, too. But he will not put himself in much danger; he will not take risks.

The warrior, the Kshatriya, takes risks. He puts his life at stake. He becomes a gambler. The businessman is never a gambler. He thinks first about the profit and he goes only so far. He takes risks, but only limited risks, and he always worries about profit and loss. The warrior risks all. He goes deep into life. That is the third stage.

The Brahmin is the highest, the one who goes deeper into the mystery of life, reality, existence. And he is never satisfied unless he comes to know what ultimate truth is. That is what Brahmin means—one who comes face-to-face with the ultimate truth, the absolute truth.

Buddha said that these are not divisions of birth, these are the qualities that you have to evolve into. Everybody has to evolve from the Sudra and everybody has to go to the Brahmin. Buddha destroyed the whole idea of the caste structure. He said that a sannyasin

has nothing to do with age or how old you are. Age has nothing to do with sannyas; it is not a chronological thing. If sannyas is not concerned with time, how can it be concerned with age? Sannyas is a movement into the timeless for anybody who is ready. Sometimes a child will enter into sannyas. Shankara entered into sannyas when he was only nine years of age. If he had waited according to the old Hindu concept, he would have never become a sannyasin, because by the age of thirty-three he was dead. Humanity would have missed something tremendous.

Buddha said that sannyas can be entered whenever somebody is ready. And there are different qualities of people, different intensities, different passions. At the age of nine, someone may be more alert than most people are, even at the age of ninety. You cannot decide outright by a person's age; you have to look into the inner intensity of the person.

It is your life. If you want to risk it, it is your freedom. You have to be allowed. Buddha allowed young people to be initiated into sannyas.

These two systems were the foundations of the Hindu society, and both were destroyed in Buddha's approach. People were against him, naturally. He was always in danger. But he created a great revolution in human consciousness.

In this story, Buddha was passing through a village of Brahmins. They gathered around him and they insulted him very much. He listened silently. They pushed and pushed

the buttons, but nothing happened. So they became a little embarrassed—when you insult somebody and he stands there unperturbed, you become embarrassed. He seems to be beyond you. In fact, you cannot reach him because he is at such a height.

They asked, "Are you listening? Why are you standing silently? We are insulting and condemning you. Have you gone dumb? Have you gone deaf? Can't you speak? Can't you hear what we are saying?"

Buddha said, "I can feel and see your worries and your embarrassment, but I am sorry. You should have come ten years earlier if you wanted me to react. Now it is too late. Now these buttons don't work. I have gone beyond them."

It is as if a child is playing with a toy and you snatch the toy away and he cries and weeps. One day he will not be a child, and then if you snatch his toy away he will not cry and weep. In fact, he will give it to you, he will present it to you and say, "You can take it, you can have it. I am finished with it."

That's what Buddha said. He said, "It is too late. I am finished with it. I have gone beyond."

This is knowing, real knowing. Knowing is a qualitative change in your being. It is a

transformation of your being, it is a metanoia. As you move higher, the altitude changes. With knowledge, the so-called knowledge, you remain the same, but you go on accumulating more. You know more—but *you* remain the same.

The so-called knowledge is like money. You hoard money—but that doesn't change you. How can it change you? Your bank balance grows, but that doesn't mean you are growing with it. You may hoard millions of dollars, but how is that going to help your growth? You remain the same. That's why you will see that even rich people remain beggars. The money

is there, but their inner beggary remains the same. They remain the same way—miserly.

Sometimes they become even more miserly, because when you don't have so much, you are not so worried about losing it. When you have it, you become worried about losing it. Rich people become poorer; their poverty is tremendous. They cannot share. They are always afraid. Their inner poverty does not change at all; it remains the same. It has to be so. If you are aggressive, changing your clothes will not make you become non-aggressive. If you are angry, changing the style of your hair will not make you peaceful. So the amount of money you have does not make any difference to your inner being.

In the same way, the amount of knowledge you have makes no difference. You can go to the university, attain all the degrees possible, visit libraries, read and study, and collect much knowledge—but it will be just on the outside, on the periphery of your mind. It will be just in your memory; it will not change the quality of your consciousness. And unless your consciousness changes, nothing is attained.

So the first thing to be understood is that knowledge and knowing are different. Knowledge is information; knowing is understanding. Knowledge is gathered from the outside; knowing is a growth inside. Knowledge is borrowed; knowing is yours, authentically yours. Knowledge is learned; knowing is not learned from anybody.

You have to become more alert so that you can see more, so that you can feel more, so that you can be more. Knowing is being; knowledge is just a peripheral accumulation.

Another thing: When you are full of knowledge, when you have hoarded much knowledge, your ego will be strengthened. You will think, "I know so much." And the ego is one of the barriers toward reality. It is not a bridge: it disconnects, it does not connect. When you are a person of knowing, ego disappears—because a person of knowing comes to know that there is nothing you can know. How can you know? Life is so mysterious, so tremendously mysterious, there is no way to truly know it.

If you can know only yourself, that is more than enough, more than anyone can expect. If a small light starts burning in your heart and your inner being becomes lighted, that is more than enough. And that is what is needed. In that light you become aware that the reality is an ultimate mystery—that's what we mean when we use the word *God*. *God* means exactly what *nature* means with only one difference. In the concept of nature it is implied that what is not known now will be known later on—but it can be known. It is knowable. That is the intrinsic meaning of nature.

Nature is theoretically knowable. Scientists talk about nature because we have known something of it, and one day everything will be known. By using the word *God* or *godliness* we bring another dimension into it. We say that something is known and more will be known—more will always be known—yet something will always remain unknowable, something will be forever elusive.

The mystery is vast; the mystery is infinite. And we are part of it—how can the part know the whole totally? It is impossible. The part cannot know the whole totally, the part can only know so far.

A person of knowing understands the mystery of life. That's why Buddha is silent about life. He does not say a single word about it.

Lao Tzu kept quiet for his whole life until he was forced to write his experiences. But the first sentence he wrote in the *Tao Te Ching* was that the Tao, the truth that can be said, is

> *Tao says that any activity can be turned into a sacred activity—any activity whatsoever, even archery, even swordsmanship.*

not the real Tao. The Tao that can be uttered or expressed is already false.

The truth cannot be said because you can say only things that have been known totally, known perfectly. Truth is never known totally. You feel it, you live it, you have great experiences of it—great visions, great mysteries open—but each mystery brings you to another mystery. As each door opens you see that a thousand and one doors are still waiting, unopened. Each door brings you to new doors. So how can you express it?

A person of knowing will say, "I don't know," or "I don't know the all, I know only a little bit. I know only myself." But that is enough—that is more than enough. That is the highest one can aspire to.

The person of knowledge claims to know everything and hence proves ignorant. Only an ignorant person claims to know; the knower always admits not knowing. That is the sign, the indication, of real knowing.

One thing more: When you know something, you divide reality into the knower, the known, and the knowledge. The reality immediately becomes divided into three things. That's the meaning of the symbol of the trinity in Christianity. If you *know*, God becomes three. The moment you know, God becomes three; the one is no longer one. Knowledge divides. That is the meaning of the concept of the *trimurti* in Hinduism—God has three faces. The moment you know, he has three faces. Knowledge divides.

It seems that three is basic. If you dissolve into reality there is one, but the moment you turn it over and look at it, it turns into three. Certainly, because then you are one thing, that which you know is another, and between the two is knowledge—the knower, the known, and the knowledge.

Knowledge divides—and that which divides cannot lead you to ultimate truth. Knowing unites. In knowing, one does not know who is the knower, who is the known, and what is knowledge. That's why in knowing, you become a mystic. In knowing, you become one with reality; in knowing, you lose all distinctions, differences, boundaries, definitions. In knowing, you become undefined—as undefined as reality itself.

Now here is a parable.

Lieh Tzu was studying archery, and hit the target. He sought advice from Kuan-Yin who asked him, "Do you know why you hit the target?"

Each word has to be understood. Have the taste of each single word—because each single word is significant. These parables are not just to be read in one stroke and forgotten about; these parables were written to meditate upon.

These are meditative devices.

Lieh Tzu was studying archery.

Tao makes no difference between the sacred and the profane. All the organized religions make a distinction between the sacred and the profane. Archery is a profane art—as is swordsmanship, or cooking, or carpentry, or painting, or poetry. You cannot think of Buddha painting and you cannot think of Buddha as an archer. You cannot even think of Buddha composing poetry. These are mundane activities; Buddha is transcendental.

Can you imagine Buddha doing any ordinary day-to-day activity? No, he simply meditates. He remains in the purest sky. He walks on the earth but he does not belong to the earth. He walks on the earth but he never touches the earth. He is not an earthly being.

But Tao is something rare and extraordinary. Tao says that any activity can be turned into a sacred activity—any activity whatsoever, even archery, even swordsmanship. In China and Japan there are schools of archery and swordsmanship, but in the hall where the archer learns archery you will find a sign: *Meditation Hall*. People learn archery or sometimes wrestling—but the hall is known as the Meditation Hall. What type of meditation is this? People are fighting, wrestling, learning archery—all murderous arts. What type of meditation is this? Why do they call these places meditation halls?

Tao says that any activity done with full awareness becomes a meditation. Activity is not the real thing—how you do it, what consciousness you bring to it, is the real

thing. You can pray in an earthly way and it will become mundane—and you know it. If you go to the temple and listen to people's prayers, you will know it. Their prayers are not real prayers. Somebody is asking to win the lottery; somebody is asking that his wife who is ill should be made well again; somebody is saying that his son has failed, next time God should please take care that he passes his exams. Somebody is saying that her daughter has grown up and it is difficult to find a boy for her—please help. These are their prayers. They are mundane activities, very ordinary. Why do you call them prayers? What is sacred about them? Nothing seems to be sacred about them. You may be sitting in a temple but that doesn't make much difference.

If prayer can be profane, then surely ordinary activities can be sacred. That is a Taoist contribution to the world. The activity is not the real thing, but the consciousness you bring to it.

Take wrestling, for example. The Taoist wrestler first has to bow down to his opponent and meditate on the opponent as being divine, an expression of godliness—not as the enemy. If he cannot meditate on the enemy as being an expression of the divine, as being a friend, then he is not Taoist. Then it is ordinary wrestling. But if he can see the same godliness in his opponent as he feels in himself, then wrestling is wrestling only on the surface; deep down it has become prayer.

If you observe from the outside, you will be puzzled. Two swordsmen fighting with their swords first have to look into one another's

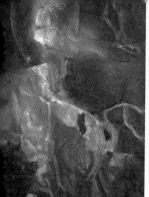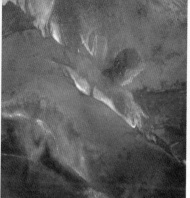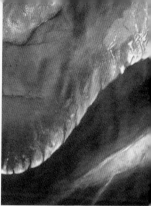

eyes, in through the window of each other's eyes, to get the feel of each other's being. It is exactly like his own being. Then when they fight, the fight is totally different. The fight is not aggressive or egoistic; the fight is a play. The wrestlers or the swordsmen are not interested in killing each other. They are not even interested in protecting themselves. They simply relax and let go. Then two energies are there, dancing. It is wrestling to you if you look from the outside, but from the inside it is just a dance of two energies. It is almost a love affair, this meeting of two energies.

And, you will be surprised to know that if somebody is defeated, that person is thought to be the one who is not yet in a let-go. He was still an egoist; that's why he was defeated.

Sometimes it happens that two Taoist wrestlers have been wrestling again and again for years and neither has been defeated—because both were non-egoists. How can you defeat a non-egoist? Both are non-aggressive. Both are in such tremendous love that neither can defeat the other. Two swordsmen may fight for hours and neither

gets hurt. This is the art. The whole art is to be so empty that the sword cannot cut anything.

Now, if somebody hits you, you shrink; if somebody hits you, you resist. The Taoist art is: when somebody hits you, you expand. You take the attack into yourself and absorb it.

If somebody is throwing energy at you, don't fight with that energy, absorb it. He is giving you energy and you are fighting with it? Absorb it instead!

Try it sometime. If somebody hits you or punches you one day, try to absorb it. Just go with it. Don't get hard, don't become stiff, let it be absorbed. You will be surprised. You will be surprised because it will be a totally new experience. If one fighter absorbs the other's energy—whatever he is throwing out—the one who is throwing out energy will be defeated. It is not that the other has defeated him—he has defeated himself. He will become weaker and weaker, and he will be defeated. The other fighter will come out of it radiant.

Every activity can be turned into meditation. Even the murderous arts of archery and fighting can be turned into nonviolent arts. This is a great revolution.

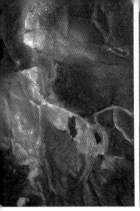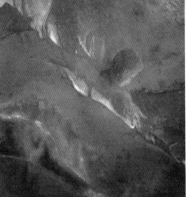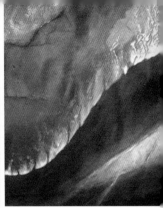

The ego is hard and masculine. Tao believes in the feminine. The ego is aggressive; the feminine is receptive. Tao believes in the receptive. Tao believes in becoming a womb. The ego, the masculine ego, is determined to penetrate rather than be penetrated. The masculine ego is always trying to penetrate the other—just as in sex.

In everything the male ego does, there is an effort at penetration, an effort to violate the other. And the feminine is absorbing —just as in sex. As in sex, so in everything.

Have you not watched it happening every day? You may not have thought about it in that way. Women are always the winners. Napoleon may be a great man outside his house, but when he comes back home he is nothing. The woman may be tiny, a wisp of a woman, but she dominates. Every husband is henpecked. If you can find a husband who is not henpecked, then know well that he is a Taoist. He is not masculine, that's why he is not henpecked. He is already feminine. Each husband has to be henpecked because the egoistic energy cannot win against the non-egoistic energy.

Have you not watched it? A woman crying is very powerful. You may have all the muscles in the world, you may be the great Mohammed Ali, but even Mohammed Ali, when his girlfriend is crying, just does not know what to do. The tears seem to be more powerful.

What is the power in the tears of a woman? She is so fragile, she is so vulnerable, she is so soft—from where comes the power of the woman? Why does she dominate, how does she manage? She manages without managing. She takes care of you; she serves you in a thousand and one ways. And that's how she becomes the conqueror. She never tries to penetrate you, she never tries to conquer you—that is her victory. She is defenseless. But still some great strength comes from some unknown source.

Taoists say that this is the strength of the water element. Man is like rock and woman is like water. When the water falls on the rocks, the rock disappears and becomes sand— sooner or later. It is only a question of time. On the first contact of the water with the rock, the rock is so strong and the water is so soft that you cannot logically imagine that one day the

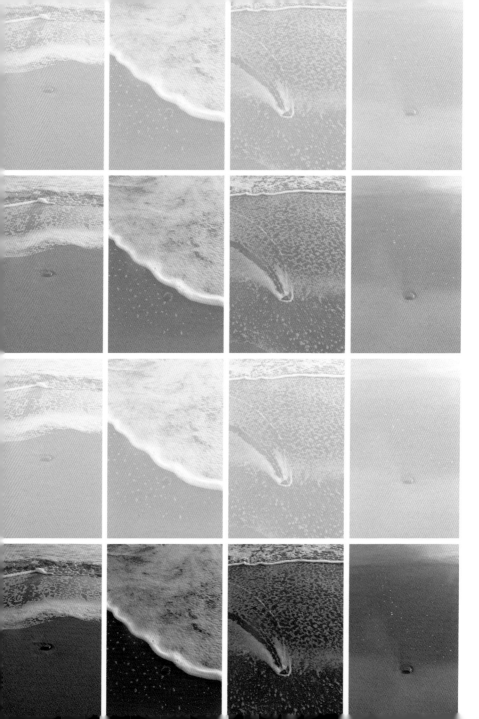

water will destroy the rock, that the rock will disappear as sand and the water will still be there.

This is what Lao Tzu calls "the watercourse way"—the strength of the feminine.

The energy of the masculine is that of the woodcutter. Have you watched a woodcutter chopping wood? That is the energy of the masculine—destructive, aggressive, violent. The feminine energy is that of the surfer. The male wrestles with life rather than swimming with it; the feminine goes with it, swims with it, does not wrestle with it. The feminine is pliant and supple, more like liquid.

If somebody is studying archery he can study it as a masculine energy. Then he will become technically expert but he will miss the deeper art of it.

Lieh Tzu was studying archery, and hit the target.

Now this is the male understanding. If you hit the target you have learned the art. What more is needed? If out of a hundred tries you can hit the target a hundred times, what more is needed?

In Japan, a German professor, Herrigel, was learning archery with a Zen master. He became perfect, one hundred percent perfect—not a single target was ever missed. Naturally he said to the master, "Now what more is there? Now what more have I to learn here? Can I go now?"

The master said, "You can go but you have not learned even the ABC of my art."

Herrigel said, "The ABC of your art? My target is one hundred percent perfect now."

The master said, "Who is talking about the

> *When the water falls on the rocks, the rock disappears and becomes sand—sooner or later. It is only a question of time.*

target? Any fool can do that just by practicing. That is nothing much. Now the real thing starts.

"When the archer takes his bow and arrow and aims at the target, there are three elements. One is the archer: the most fundamental and basic thing, the source, the innermost. Then there is the arrow that will pass from the archer to the target. And then there is the bullseye: the target, the farthest—away thing. If you hit the target you have touched the farthest, you have touched the periphery. You have to touch the source. You can become technically expert in hitting the target, but that is not much—not much if you are trying to get into deeper waters. You are an expert, you are a man of knowledge, but not a man of knowing.

"The arrow moves from you—but you don't know from with what energy the arrow moves. How does it move? Who is moving it? You don't know that. You don't know the archer. Archery you have studied, the target you have achieved, a hundred percent perfect was your aim, at a hundred percent perfection level you have become efficient—but this is about the target. What about you? What about the archer? Has anything happened in the archer? Has your consciousness changed a little bit? No, nothing has changed. You are a technician; you are not a real artist."

Taoists say that the real thing is to see the source of the aim from where this arrow takes the energy. Who is it that has succeeded? What is the energy? What being is hidden behind you? That is the real target. If that is the target and sometimes you miss the outer target, it's not a problem.

It is said about a great archer in Japan that he always used to miss his target. He was the greatest master, but he was never able to aim rightly. What was his mastery? His mastery was of a totally different kind. He had penetrated into the source; he had made the target his center.

The periphery is not the point. You may succeed or you may fail, but that is not the point at all. The real thing is: have you succeeded in becoming centered in your being? Has that target been achieved?

To succeed with the outer target is the masculine energy, to succeed with your inner source is the feminine energy. To succeed with the outer source you have to be aggressive, ambitious, concentrated, attentive, outgoing, extrovert—the arrow will be going out, will be going away from you. The arrow will be going into the world.

To move into your center you need to be feminine, passive, inactive, nondoing, noninterfering, *wu-wei* meditative. Meditation and relaxation, not concentration, are needed.

You have to relax yourself completely and utterly. When you are not doing anything, then you are at your center; when you are doing something, you have gone away. When you do too much you are far away. Coming closer means dropping your activities, learning how to be inactive, learning how to be a non-doer.

Herrigel's master said to him, "You have become a doer, a perfect doer, but that is not the point. That you could have learned in Germany, there was no need to come to Japan. Masculine arts are available in the West. But if you have come to the East, then please learn the real thing. Now you have to take your bow without being a doer; you have to pull your arrow without being a puller; you have to aim at the target without aiming. There should be no tension, no effort, no doing on your part. Just be passive. Let it happen rather than doing it. Then you will be centered."

Do you know the difference between doing a thing and letting it happen? If you know the difference, then you can understand this parable, otherwise, it will be difficult.

Let me remind you, because you may not have noted it. Sometimes, making love, you were a doer. Then you missed. Yes, there was a sexual release, but it was not a true orgasm. Sometimes it was not a doing, you allowed it to happen—then it was a release, certainly, but with a plus. It was an orgasm. You had a feeling of expansion, you became enormous and huge; you touched the very boundaries of existence. In that moment you disappeared as an ego; you were not. You pulsated from one core to another core, you pulsated in all your layers, but you were not the doer. Bring the doer in, and the pulsation stops. Drop the doer and the pulsation starts again.

Sometimes, swimming in a river, you start floating. Swimming is beautiful, but nothing compared with floating. Sometimes, just lying in the river, not making any effort, you start floating with the river—then you know a totally different quality of experience. The river takes you in her arms, the river supports you, the river and you are no longer enemies—there is a sort of inner connectedness. You have fallen *en rapport* with the river energy; your energy and the energy of the river are making love. Then there is an orgasm.

Sometimes, sitting silently, doing nothing, you have become aware of letting go. And there is a benediction. Sometimes, looking at the stars or at the trees, suddenly it is there. You were not doing anything.

These moments come to everybody. They come when you are not expecting them, they come only when you are *not*; they steal in when your doors are open and you are relaxed. Sometimes out of nothingness and from nowhere a great benediction comes. These moments come to everybody, but you have not observed them, you have not noticed them. These are gifts from existence. They are reminders: "You are in a strange land—come back home." Existence knocks on your heart again and again—whenever an opportunity is there, whenever you allow it.

On a Sunday you can lie in bed, not in any hurry to go to the office, and the children are awake and rushing around the room and your

partner is preparing the tea and there is the sound of the kettle, and the traffic slowly moving outside, and you turn in your bed and you pull your blanket up again and there is nowhere to go—it is Sunday. Christianity has given one beautiful thing to the world—Sunday. Hinduism has no Sunday. Sunday is the greatest contribution of Christianity. You can dream a little more; you can float into sleep again. There are scents from the kitchen, breakfast is being made, and you are in a state of relaxation, not tense, —and suddenly you feel tremendously beautiful. Life has meaning. Something flowers in you. Something unknown enters you. These are the moments when you are feminine.

Rushing to the office you become male. You may walk on the street along which you go to the office every day—but when you are just going for a walk, you are a female. When you are going for a walk, you are not going anywhere in particular, you are just enjoying the birds in the trees and the wind and the morning and the sun and the children laughing and going to school. You are enjoying, not going anywhere in particular, and at any point you can turn back home; there is no target, there is no goal, you are simply enjoying a morning walk—and suddenly it is there, that moment of let-go.

Watch these moments of let-go, because they are messages from the beyond. Watch these moments of let-go: cherish them, taste them. Welcome them so that they become more and more available to you. Receive the guest gratefully so that it will come more and more often.

Tao says that the real happens only when you are in such a state of diffused relaxedness that you cannot say "I am." "I am" means you are tense.

Lieh Tzu was studying archery, and he hit the target. He sought advice from Kuan Yin who asked him, "Do you know why you hit the target?"

Kuan Yin is a Taoist master and an archer. Lieh Tzu said, "I have become an expert. Technically, I have attained my goal. I have hit the target."

The master asked, "Do you know why you hit the target?" From where? Who are you? Who is this one that has hit the target? Have you looked deep into the source of your energies? Forget the target and look at the archer. Archery you have learned, what about the archer? Now you have to learn the archer. And the processes are very different. You have learned archery, but if you want to learn the archer you will have to unlearn archery."

By learning, you know the world; by unlearning, you know yourself. By learning, you accumulate knowledge; by unlearning, you become a knower. By learning, you hoard; by unlearning, you become nude, empty.

The master asked, "Do you know why you hit the target?" Why did he ask? That's what Socrates means when he says to his disciples that an unexamined life is not worth living. You may succeed, but your life is not worth living if it has not been examined so deeply that you know the source of it, the very foundation of it.

You see the flowers of a tree, but that is not real knowledge unless you go deep enough to know the roots. The flowers depend on the roots. The flowers are nothing but the innermost core of the roots, come to be expressed. The roots are carrying the poetry, the source, the juice, which will become flowers, which will become fruits, which will become leaves. And if you continually count the leaves and the flowers and the fruits and never go deep into the darkness of the earth, you will never understand the tree because the tree is in the roots.

Where are the roots of the archer? You have succeeded in hitting the target—that is a flowering—but where are your roots? Do you know why you hit the target? Do you know why these flowers have bloomed? Do you know from what source? The flower is the last activity, the most peripheral. The roots are the seed, the primary activity, the most basic. The roots can exist without the flowers, but the flowers cannot exist without the roots. You can cut the flowers off and another flower will come; in fact, a far better flower will come. If you cut the flower, the roots will take up the challenge immediately and they will send a bigger flower. They will say, "Let us see who wins."

I once had a gardener, a very rare man, a master-gardener, who used to win all the competitions in the city. Nobody was ever able to produce such big flowers as he—all sorts of flowers. I asked him, "What is your secret?"

He said, "This is my secret: I challenge the roots."

I said, "What do you mean?"

He said, "I cut the flowers. I don't allow ordinary flowers to happen to the tree at all. If the tree can give a hundred flowers, I allow only one. Ninety-nine I drop; I cut them off immediately because they are a waste. And the roots get madder and madder and angrier and angrier. And then comes the biggest flower—as if all one hundred flowers were made into one. Finally, the roots win. That is my secret: I make them mad."

You can cut the flower and it will come again; cut another and it will be replaced. But cut the roots and the tree is gone.

The master asked, "Do you know why you hit the target?" The disciple said, without any hesitation, without waiting for a single moment, "No." This is honesty. The disciple is really a disciple. It is Lieh Tzu himself, the man we have been talking about all this time. He said, "No." This is honesty.

If I ask you, "Do you know who you are?" only the very honest will say, "No." The dishonest will start brooding; the dishonest will say, "Let me think about it." What are you going to think about? If you know, you know; if you don't know, you don't know. What are you going to think about? Thinking means you will try to manage an answer, you will try to manufacture an answer. It is difficult to find a person who can admit that they don't know. And that is the one who can become a real disciple; that is the one who one day can know.

You will not say, "No." Somebody will say, "Yes, God exists. I know," and somebody else will say "I know there is no God"—but both know. Few are able to say, "I don't know."

Lieh Tzu said "No"—he is a real disciple, a true disciple, authentic. The disciple has to open his heart before the master—the disciple has to be nude. He cannot hide anything, because if you hide from the master you will never grow.

Lieh Tzu said, "No."

Then the Master said, "It won't do yet. It is good, you have progressed, and your no is a good indication, but it won't do yet. You have to go further still.

He went away to practice and after three years again reported to Kuan Yin.

What did Lieh Tzu do for three years? He had attained his target, so what was he doing for three years? The parable does not say, because this is a parable to be meditated upon. A parable is such that it says only a few things and leaves many things unsaid, so that you have to meditate and fill in the gaps. You have to find where the intervals are. And in those intervals lies the real thing.

What did he do for three years? When you have hit the target, what more can you do? He was unlearning. Learning was finished; learning was complete—so he was unlearning, or he was turning his eyes inward.

Watch. When an archer takes the bow and the arrow in his hand his eyes are on the target, naturally. So what was Lieh Tzu doing for three years? When he took up his bow and arrow he would look at the target, but deep down he would look at himself. The target became secondary. The arrow of his consciousness became a double-arrow—that's what Gurdjieff calls self-remembering.

When you look at me, you are seeing me; your consciousness is one-arrowed, aimed toward me. If you change.... This you can do right now, and it will be right to do it in order to understand. You are looking at me; your eyes are on me. If you are focused on me you will forget

道

道

yourself. This is a kind of forgetfulness. Now make your consciousness a double-arrow: Look at me and at the same time, simultaneously, look at yourself. Look at the seen and look at the seer.

When you are listening to someone, listen—but always become aware of the listener, too. The talker has to be listened to and the listener also has to be listened to. Then your consciousness has double arrows. Right now it is one-way traffic: you look at me and you are not looking at yourself. This is a sort of self-forgetfulness. If you look at me and simultaneously become capable of looking at yourself, in that moment self-awareness happens.

What Lieh Tzu did for three years in the forest was a harder task. Learning was simple. He was male. Now he had to become female. First he was trying to penetrate the target outside; now he started moving inside, into the womb of his own being. He became feminine.

Knowledge is aggression; knowing is passivity.

There are two types of mind mentioned in Tao: one they call *mui* and the other they call *ui*. *Mui* means "natural, relaxed," and *ui* means "unnatural, tense." When you are fighting with life you exist as *ui*; when you are flowing with life you exist as *mui*. Swimming, you function as *ui*; floating, you function as *mui*.

When you are in a let-go, it is the natural mind in tune with the whole, in tune with Tao. Then the birds singing are not a distraction— on the contrary, they enrich the silence. Then everything is allowed. All the doors are open. You are not resisting, you are not struggling, you simply are. That is the state of *mui*.

First Lieh Tzu learned and created the state of *ui*: he became aggressive, extroverted, pointed toward the outside. It was ambition. He succeeded; he fulfilled his target. Then the master said this was nothing, he had to go further. Then what did he do for three years? He became *mui*: he relaxed. He would sit silently and feel the let-go. And by and by, he would take his arrow and bow and release the arrow in a state of let-go. He would not shoot it—he would allow it to be shot. That is difficult. He would not shoot it—he would wait for it to shoot itself.

Herrigel tried with his master but could not succeed. Then one day, desperate, he said, "I don't think I will ever be able to succeed. I cannot understand what you call this mui; it is all nonsense. How can the arrow shoot itself if I don't shoot it? If I don't pull the bow, how can things happen on their own? It is impossible."

We can understand Herrigel. That is the Western attitude: "It is impossible."

The master said, "Then you can go."

Herrigel asked, "Will you give me a certificate?"

The master said, "Impossible, because you have not learned anything. Whatsoever you have learned you could have learned anywhere else, so it is of no significance that you were here. You can go." So Herrigel booked a flight, made the arrangements to leave, forgot all about everything. He had been there for three years—it was too long.

He went to say goodbye to the master, but the master was teaching other disciples so he had to wait. He sat on a bench while the master was teaching and for the first time he was in a relaxed state because now he was no longer worried—he was leaving, it was finished—and he was no longer greedy. There was no effort. He just looked—and he could see that the master was not shooting. The master took the bow in his hand, and he pulled on the bow with his hand—but the arrow shot itself. He could see it—it was a vision. How he had missed it up to now, he could not believe!

For three years he had been watching his master again and again, but his own logical mind had been an interference. It would not allow him to see. He said, "How can it be? He may be more of an expert, but how can it be that the arrow goes by itself?" This morning he could see it. Now he was relaxed. Now he was not worried about attaining anything When you are no longer engaged in effort, greed, or desire, you are relaxed.

He rushed to the master, touched his feet, and without saying anything took the bow from his hand and shot the arrow. And the master put his hand on his head and said, "You have done it. You can have the certificate. And you can still go because now there is no need to wait. Finished. You have known it, you have tasted it."

Things can happen on their own. You were born—you did not manage it. You fell in love—you did not do it. Hunger comes, you eat and feel satisfied. Thirst arises, you drink and feel quenched. You are young; you will become old. One day you will die. Everything is happening. The doer is a false illusion. Be in the state of *mui*.

The society creates the state of *ui*. It makes you unnatural, tense, knowledgeable; it makes you cultivated, cultured—but it creates a hard crust around your heart and you lose your real nature, Tao.

He went away to practice and after three years again reported to Kuan Yin. "Do you know why you hit the target?"—again the same question—"*I know,*" said Lieh Tzu. Again it is simple—as simple as the first "No." It is not a pretension. When a person pretends, he thinks before he says, "I know." He tries to rehearse it in his mind—that's what you call thinking. The answer is without any thinking on Lieh Tzu's part. It is as it is. First he said simply, "No." Now, in exactly the same humble way—with no claim, remember—he says, "I know."

Many times you get too involved in words. The Upanishads say that one who says "I know" does not know. Right—but there can be a person who says, "I know," and does know. If you can say, "I know," in a simple, humble way, with no claim, then there is no problem. When the Upanishads say that if a person says, "I know" he does not know, the emphasis of the Upanishadic seer is on the *I*. When somebody says, "I know" the emphasis is on the *I*; it is underlined. When a person *really* knows and says, "I know," the *I* is not underlined. The "know" is just a fact. How can Lieh Tzu say something untrue? If he knows, he knows. He has to say it. But it is not a claim.

So don't get too burdened with words. People do get burdened with words. For example, if a Vedantin reads this he will say, "He says 'I know' so he cannot know because of what the Upanishads say." Words are words, and one has to feel the innermost core of the words, the heart of the words.

When Lieh Tzu says "I know," he knows. And his "I know" means exactly the same as when the Upanishads say, "I don't know." It means exactly the same as when Socrates says, "I don't know a thing." By saying, "I don't know a thing," Socrates is denying the *I*. But by saying, "I know," as a simple fact, as an ordinary fact, with no claim, Lieh Tzu is doing a far greater miracle because—listen to it—sometimes a pretender can pretend and say, "I don't know," in the hope that you will think that he knows. Because the Upanishads say so and Socrates says so, a pretender can say, "I don't know," in the hope that you will think that he is a knower, that he is another Socrates. Mind is very cunning. So remember one thing: if a mind is simple, humble, and simply states the fact, then that is the truth—whatsoever the fact.

"It will do," said the master.

Very easily he said, "It will do." It is not a question of what Lieh Tzu is saying, it is a question of what Lieh Tzu is—the simplicity, humbleness, meekness of the person, the innocence of the person. When you say, "I know," a subtle ego arises. Just say the words "I know" and you will feel a subtle ego strengthening in you.

The master must have been looking into Lieh Tzu. Masters don't look at you, they look into you. They don't watch your face, they watch your heart. He must have looked into the heart when Lieh Tzu said, "I know." Did something arise there? Did something integrate, become an ego? Nothing. The space remained untouched, virgin. He said, "I know" and nothing happened inside him. The master said:

"It will do. Hold on to this awareness and do not lose it."

It is difficult to gain a glimpse of this let-go and it is easy to lose it, because for centuries, for many lives, we have practiced doing. When those moments of nondoing come, our whole

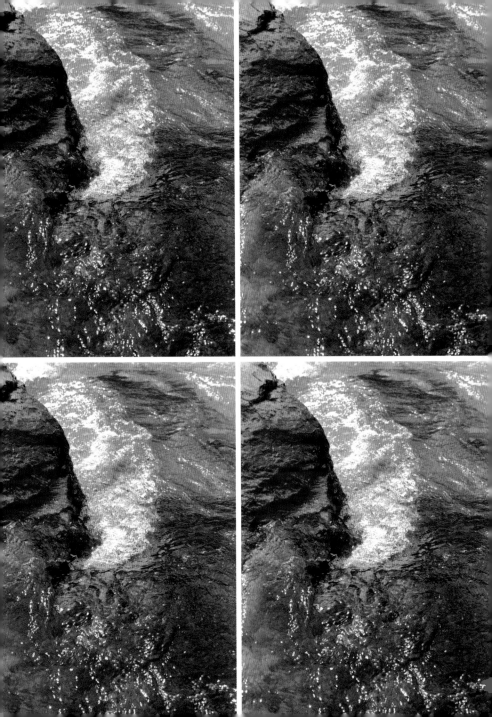

practice of many lives is against them; our habit is against them, our whole mechanism is against them. Their happening is a breakthrough and your past will struggle to close your doors again.

That's why the master says, "Hold on to this awareness and do not lose it." This is the treasure, the kingdom of God within you. This is the treasure—to be in a relaxed state and allow Tao to function. Now Lieh Tzu was not doing anything. Yes, he took the bow, he took the arrow, he aimed at the target, but he was not—it was Tao in him.

This applies not only to archery, but also to ruling oneself: therefore, the sage scrutinizes not the fact of survival or ruin, but its reasons.

"This applies not only to archery but to ruling oneself"—in fact, in Tao and Zen, archery is just a way to learn something about life. When somebody insults you, remember that the person who has insulted you is outside you, on the periphery, like the target. You are

deep within yourself, the source. And between you and the insulter stands the mind—like the arrow.

If your mind is arrowed on the person who has insulted you, you will miss. Let it be arrowed toward the source. Rather than thinking that he has insulted you, look into your own being: you must be carrying some wound, that's why you feel insulted. Otherwise, how can anybody insult you?

If somebody calls you a fool and you feel insulted that simply means you think that you are wise—nothing else. If you yourself think you are a fool, you will hug the person. You will say, "Right! Exactly right! That's how I feel!" Then where is the insult?

If somebody says you are a thief and you feel humiliated, that simply means that you have been thinking that you are a great moralist, virtuous, this and that—but deep down you know also that you are a thief. He has hit the sore spot in your being, a fragile point. So now there are two possibilities: either you jump on him and prove that you are not a thief, or you look inside yourself.

Always go to the source. In yoga, going to the source is called *pratyahara*. Mahavira calls this going to the source *pratikramana*. Jesus calls it "repent." Christians have misunderstood this concept. *Repent* has nothing to do with repentance. Repent originally meant, "return, go back, go inside yourself." The Greeks have the right word for it: *metanoia*—turn into yourself, take a 180-degree turn. You must have seen in some old ancient mystery books the symbol of a snake eating its own tail—that is *metanoia*.

Go back to yourself. Rather than going to the other, turn back and go to yourself. Let your arrow move in a circle and come back to the source from where it started. Somebody has insulted you and turmoil arises—this is the beginning of the arrow. The arrow starts moving toward the other person. It wants to hit the other person, to insult the other person. Don't be deceived by it. Let it move in a circle. Let it come 180 degrees back to you—to where it started, to where you felt the turmoil. Let it come back; look there.

This can become the key for an inner transformation. A new being is possible. Archery is just a device. Taoists have created many devices. But in all devices the basic thing, the essential thing, is to turn to your own nature.

Meditate on this parable and start using it in your life. First, look for moments of letting go. Wait for them and receive them with great welcome and rejoicing. Invite them again and again. Become more feminine.

Second, if any opportunity arises when your arrow starts to move outward, remember immediately and turn it inward. Turn it in. Rather than turning on, turn in! If somebody insults and you are turned on, if a beautiful woman passes by and you are turned on and sex arises—turn in rather than turning on. A beautiful woman passing by is not the real target: you have some sexuality in you. Go to the source. Let it be a great opportunity for meditation. Transform each ordinary opportunity into meditation and great will be the payoff. Each moment will become luminous.

Remember that there is no mundane or profane activity. All activities can be turned into meditation—they have to be. This is my message, too. Meditation must not be something apart from life; it has to become the innermost core of it. Each activity, small and great, has to be luminous with meditative awareness. Then you will see that each activity brings you to your innermost core, each activity brings you home, each activity becomes a liberation.

Each activity has to fall back into the original source. The anger that arises from your being has to fall back into your being; the sex that arises from your being has to fall back to the source itself. There, where the alpha and the omega meet, where the beginning and the end meet, where the snake turns to its own tail and starts eating it, you become complete, a whole circle. That's the stage of the sage.

ko hsuan:
no doctrine, no teaching

Consciousness is experienced only when you are unconditioned and not reconditioned again, when you are left alone to yourself, utterly innocent. One can call it purity. That's the essence of Ko Hsuan's Tao. The verses of Ko Hsuan are called The Classic of Purity. Tao has no doctrines, no teachings. It believes in absolute emptiness of the mind, in nothingness. When you are utterly empty you come in contact with the beyond. The beyond is not far away, but you are so full of rubbish, so full of junk, that there is no space for the beyond to enter in you. It is like a room is full of furniture. Empty the room of all furniture: on the one hand the room is emptied, all furniture is removed from the room; on the other hand the room is becoming full of emptiness, the sky is entering, the space is entering—the room is becoming more spacious. That's what happens when your being is unconditioned and left alone.

道

the classic of purity

The Classic of Purity is one of the most profound insights into nature. I call it an insight—not a doctrine, not a philosophy, not a religion—because it is not intellectual at all; it is existential. The man who is speaking in it is not speaking from the mind. He is not speaking as himself, either; he is an empty passage for existence itself to say something through him.

THAT'S HOW THE great mystics have always lived and spoken. These are not their own words—they are no more, they have disappeared long before— it is the whole pouring through them. Their expressions may be different, but the source is the same. The words of Jesus, Zarathustra, Buddha, Lao Tzu, Krishna, and Mohammed are not ordinary words. They are not coming from the memory; they are coming from experience. They have touched the beyond, and the moment you touch the beyond you evaporate: you cannot exist any more. You have to die for God to be.

This is a Taoist insight. Tao is another name for God, far more beautiful than God, because the word *God* has been exploited too much by the priests. They have exploited in the name of God for so long that even the word has become contaminated. Anyone of intelligence is bound to avoid it because it reminds you of all the nonsense that has happened on the earth down the ages in the name of God, in the name of religion. More mischief has happened in the name of God than in any other name.

Tao in that sense is tremendously beautiful. You cannot worship Tao because Tao does not give you any idea of a person. It is a principle, not a person. You cannot worship a principle— you cannot pray to Tao. It would look ridiculous, it would be utterly absurd to pray to a principle. You don't pray to the law of gravity; you cannot pray to the theory of relativity.

Tao is the ultimate principle that binds the whole of existence together. Existence is not chaos; that much is certain. It is a cosmos. There is immense order in it, an intrinsic order in it, and the name of that order is Tao.

Tao simply means the harmony of the whole. No temples have been built for Tao: no statues, no prayers, no priests, no rituals— that's the beauty of it. Hence, you cannot call it a doctrine, nor can you call it a religion. It is a pure insight. You can call it Dharma; that is Buddha's word for Tao. The word in English that comes closest to Tao is *Nature*, with a capital N.

This profound insight of Ko Hsuan is also one of the smallest treatises ever written. It is condensed—as if millions of roses have been condensed into one drop of perfume. That's the ancient way of expressing truth: because books were not in existence, people had to remember it.

It is said that Ko Hsuan's *Classic of Purity* is the one of the first mystic treatises ever set down in book form. It is not much of a book; not more than a couple of pages, but it existed for hundreds of years before it was written. It existed through private and personal communion. That has been always the most significant way to transmit truth. To write it down makes it more difficult because then one never knows who will be reading it; it loses all the immediacy of personal contact and touch.

In Egypt, in India, in China, in all the ancient civilizations, for thousands of years, the mystic message was carried from one person to another, from the master to the disciple. And the master would say these things only when the disciple was ready, or he would say only as much as the disciple could digest.

For centuries all the mystics resisted writing down their insights. This was the first treatise ever written; that's its significance. It marks a certain change in human consciousness, a change that was going to prove of great importance later on, because even though it is beautiful to commune directly, person to person, the message cannot reach many people; many are bound to miss. True, if it is not written down it will not fall into the wrong hands, but many right hands will also remain empty. And one should think more of the right hands than of the wrong hands. The wrong people are going to be wrong whether some profound insight falls into their hands or not, but the right people will be missing something that can transform their being.

Ko Hsuan, who wrote this small treatise, marks a milestone in the consciousness of humanity. He understood the significance of the written word, knowing all its dangers. In the preface he writes: "Before writing down these words I contemplated ten thousand times whether to write or not, because I was taking a dangerous step." Nobody had gathered that much courage before. But he also says, "Ten thousand times I contemplated," because it is no ordinary matter.

Even a man like Buddha contemplated for seven days before uttering a single word. When he attained enlightenment, for seven days he remained utterly silent, wavering about whether to say anything or not. His question was: "Those who cannot understand, what is the point of talking to them about such profound insights? They will misunderstand. They will misinterpret and do harm to the message. Rather than allowing the message to heal them, they will wound the message itself—they will manipulate the message according to their own minds and prejudices. Is it right to allow the message to be polluted by foolish people, by mediocre people, by ignorant people?"

Buddha was very hesitant. Yes, he also thought of the few people who would be able to understand it, but then he could see: "Those people who are able to understand my words will be able to find truth on their own, because they cannot be ordinary people. They would have to be the most intelligent people; otherwise, they would not be able to understand what I am saying to them. If they can understand my words they will be able to find their own way, they will be able to reach the truth on their own, so why bother about them? Maybe it will take a little longer for them. So what? Because there is eternity, time is not short. But the message, once it gets into the wrong hands, will be corrupted forever." Even to utter anything at all, Buddha was hesitant.

I can understand Ko Hsuan contemplating over the matter ten thousand times—whether to write it down or not—because when you *say* something to people, if they are stupid they are bound to forget it very soon. If they are mediocre people they will not bother even

> *Unless you have tasted something of no-mind, you cannot understand a paradox.*

to listen; they won't care. But once it is written down then they will read it, study it. Then it will become part of their schools, colleges, and universities, and scholars will ponder over it and they will write great scholarly treatises on it. People who know nothing will be talking about it for centuries and the truth will be lost in all that noise that scholars make. They will argue for and against it.

It is said that once a disciple of the devil ran to him and said, "What are you doing sitting here under this tree? Have you not heard?— one man has found the truth! We have to do something, and urgently, because if this man has found the truth our existence is in danger. Our profession is in danger—he can cut our very roots!"

The old devil laughed. He said, "Calm down, please. You are new, that's why you are so disturbed by it. Don't be worried. I have got my people, they have already started working."

The disciple said, "But I have not seen any of our people there."

The devil said, "I work in many ways. Scholars are there, pundits are there, philosophers are there, and theologians are there. Don't be worried. They will make so much noise for and against, they will create so much argumentation, that the still small voice of truth will be silenced by them. We need not worry. These scholars and pundits and these professors are my people: I work through them—they are in my service, they are my secret agents. Don't be worried. You may not have seen my disciples there, because I have to go in disguise. But I have arrived there and my people have started working—they have surrounded the person; he cannot do any harm. And soon he will be dead—he is old—and then my people will be his apostles, his priests, and they will manage the whole affair."

Priests are in the service of the devil, not in the service of God. The so-called great scholars who go on and on with logic-chopping, hair-splitting arguments are in the service of the devil, not in the service of God. Once you write down something you are giving a chance to these people; they won't miss the opportunity. They will mess the whole thing up; they will create great confusion around it. That is their expertise.

Hence, I can understand Ko Hsuan contemplating ten thousand times whether to write or not. But finally he decided to write and I think he did the right thing. One should never be afraid of darkness. Light, however small, is far more powerful than darkness, however big, however old.

In fact, darkness has no power. Light has power. These words are powerful words. The way the mystics speak the truth, it is almost beyond the scholars; they cannot destroy its beauty. In fact, they cannot even touch its truth; it is impossible for the simple reason that the mystics speak in a paradoxical language. They don't speak logically; thus, they are beyond the grasp of the scholars. The scholars can only see contradictions, because the scholar functions through logic and all the mystic expressions are paradoxical—illogical or supralogical. Taoist sayings in particular are superb in that way; nobody has been able to sort out their paradoxes. Even in this small treatise there are paradoxes almost in every sentence, in every utterance.

That, too, has to be understood. Why do mystics speak in paradox? To remain unavailable to the scholars. The paradox can be understood only by a meditator; it can never be understood by a person who lives in the head, in the mind. Unless you have tasted something of the no-mind, you cannot understand a paradox. That is a safeguard, an inbuilt safeguard. Speak paradoxically, speak as if you are almost mad.

Once a journalist went to see George Gurdjieff. Gurdjieff was drinking his morning tea. He always avoided journalists because they are the most mediocre people around, and his way of avoiding them was unique. He asked the woman who was pouring tea for him, as the journalist sat by his side, "What day is it today?"

The woman said, "Today is Saturday."

Gurdjieff went into a rage and threw the cup on the floor. The cup was shattered into thousands of pieces. The journalist became very much afraid...because it was Saturday, and Gurdjieff said, "You are always talking nonsense to me! Just the other day you were telling me that it was Friday and now today it is Saturday? How can it be? How can Saturday come after Friday?"

The journalist thought this man was mad. He escaped without even saying goodbye, and Gurdjieff had a good laugh. He said, "Now this man will never come back; I have put him off for his whole life. He will go and spread rumors about me to his professional colleagues, so not only has he been thrown out, many more who might have bothered me will never come here." He was thought to be a madman, utterly mad.

The paradoxical statements of the mystics have a purpose. The purpose is so that the scholars will avoid them. The moment the scholars come across a mystic, deep down they will believe that this person is mad and they won't waste their time.

Secondly, paradox is the only way to indicate something that is true. Logic is always half, it never takes in the whole, it cannot take in the whole. Life consists of polarities: just as electricity consists of positive and negative poles, the whole of life consists of polarities. And polarities are only *apparently* opposite to each other; deep down they are not. Deep down, for those who understand, for those who have the intelligence to see that deeply, they are not opposites, they are complementaries.

But for that you will need a deep experience of meditation; the mind alone won't help. The mind will say, "These are contradictory statements. This person is saying one thing at the beginning of the sentence but by the end of the sentence has uttered just the opposite." But the mystic knows what he is doing: he is trying to put the whole truth in what he is saying. The whole truth can be understood only by a person who has tasted something of the whole.

Mind always splits things; it divides, it separates, it functions like a prism. When a white sunray passes through the prism, it is divided into seven colors. That's how a rainbow is created: it is created by small drops of water hanging in the air. Those drops of water function like prisms and the sunrays passing through them are divided into seven colors. The mind is a prism; it divides one thing into many. The truth is one, but if you look through the mind, it appears to be many. The mystic's way of saying things is such that he wants to put all the colors of the rainbow back together again as they were in the beginning before they passed through the prism.

Because of this paradoxical way of expression, scholars avoid the mystics. People who live in the mind cannot comprehend them; it is a safeguard. That's how such beautiful treatises have survived for centuries.

Ko Hsuan is simply writing it, remember; he is not the creator of the treatise. He has also experienced the same truth, because the truth

> *The mind is a prism; it divides one thing into many. The truth is one.*

is always the same, whoever experiences it. Whenever one experiences it, it is always the same; it does not change; time makes no difference. But what he is saying has been transferred by word of mouth for hundreds, maybe thousands of years. That's why we don't exactly know whose words they are.

He begins like this:

The venerable master said:

The supreme Tao is formless, yet it produces and nurtures heaven and earth.

The supreme Tao has no desires, yet by its power the sun and moon revolve in their orbits.

The supreme Tao is nameless, yet it ever supports all things.

I do not know its name but for title call it Tao.

The venerable master said... Who is this master? Nothing is said about him. Perhaps the master simply represents all the masters of the past and all the masters of the present and all the masters of the future. Maybe it simply represents the essential wisdom—not any particular person, but simply the principle.

Nothing is known about Ko Hsuan, nothing at all. Hence, for a few centuries it had been thought that these words belonged to Lao Tzu.

But Lao Tzu has a different way of speaking, a totally different way; these words can't be coming from Lao Tzu. We have gone into the words of Lao Tzu; he is even more mad than Ko Hsuan, he is even more mystical. And it is a well-known fact that he never wrote anything other than the *Tao Te Ching*, and that he wrote under pressure, at the last moment, when he was leaving China to die in the Himalayas.

He had decided to die in the mountains, and you cannot find a more beautiful place to die than the Himalayas—the silence of the Himalayas, the virgin silence, the beauty, nature in its most profound splendor. So when he became very old he said to his disciples, "I am going to the Himalayas to find a place where I can disappear into nature, where nobody will know about me, where no monument will be made in honor of me, no temple, not even a grave. I simply want to disappear as if I had never existed."

When he was passing through the country he was stopped at the border because the king had alerted all the borders and ordered that, "If Lao Tzu passes out of the country through any gate he should be prevented unless he writes down what he has experienced." His whole life Lao Tzu had avoided this. In the end, it is said, because he was caught on the border and they wouldn't allow him to go to the Himalayas, he stayed in a guard's hut for three days and wrote down the small treatise, *Tao Te Ching*.

So it cannot be that *The Classic of Purity* belongs to Lao Tzu. But because nothing much is known about Ko Hsuan, people used to think that it must be the words of Lao Tzu, and that

Ko Hsuan must have been a disciple of Lao Tzu who simply wrote them down—the notes of a disciple. That's not so. Ko Hsuan himself is a master in his own right.

In the preface to his treatise, he says a few things that have to be remembered. First he says, "When I attained to union with Tao, I meditated upon this insight ten thousand times before writing it down." He says, "When I attained union with Tao..." He is not just a disciple; he is an enlightened man. He has attained union with Tao. He is not writing notes on what he heard from somebody else, he has experienced it himself. He has attained to the ultimate union with Tao; he has become one with nature.

He says in the preface, "It is only for the seekers of the beyond; the worldly cannot understand it." He makes it clear in the preface that if you are a worldly person, it is not meant for you, it will not be of any use to you. It may even confuse you and distract you from your worldly affairs. Don't waste your time. It is better not to get involved with things in which you are not really interested. It is better not to be accidental.

There are many people who are accidental, who are just "by the way." They will meet somebody and become interested. These people are like driftwood: they simply move with any wave; they are at the mercy of the winds, having no sense of direction.

Ko Hsuan says, "It is only for the seekers of the beyond." He makes it clear that if you are a seeker of the beyond, if you are ready to risk, then move forward, because the search for the

> *The first thing to decide is whether there is a deep longing in you to know the truth.*

beyond is risky. It is the greatest adventure, tremendously ecstatic, but not easy at all; it is arduous. It has its ecstasy and it has its agonies—it has its own cross. Of course, resurrection comes through it, but the resurrection cannot happen unless you are crucified. So he makes it clear that it is only for the seekers.

You have to be certain about yourself, whether you are a seeker or not. Are you interested in truth?—because every child is distracted from the very beginning. Few children seem to be interested in God, but so many parents force the idea of God on their children. If by chance you happen to be born into a family of atheists, then they impose the idea of atheism on you. If you are born in a communist country then, of course, communism will be imposed upon you. If not the Bible, then *Das Kapital*. If not the holy trinity, then the trinity of Marx, Engels, and Lenin, but something is bound to be imposed upon you.

No parent is loving enough to leave you alone to yourself to grow, to help you, to nourish you, and to give you total freedom to be yourself, authentically yourself. Hence, there are many people who think they are seekers of God—but they are not. Their seeking is an imposed phenomenon, a conditioning. If you are searching for God only because you have been told again and again to do it, then the word has become a reality in you but it is not part of you. It is not intrinsic; it has come from the outside and you are just like a parrot—or perhaps parrots are more intelligent than you are.

An overly enthusiastic Italian communist finds a parrot that can sing the popular communist song, "Bandiera Rosa." He buys it and takes it home, but after a few days the wife can no longer stand it. The parrot keeps singing the song all day long.

In a moment of rage she knocks the parrot over and then covers it with a cloth. When the husband comes back she tells him everything.

In despair the man lifts the cloth to see how the parrot is.

Opening one eye the parrot whispers, "Hey, comrade, are those dirty fascists gone?"

Even parrots are more intelligent than so-called human beings, who simply repeat clichés that have been handed over to them by their parents, priests, and teachers, schools, colleges, universities. This society conditions you in a certain way, and after twenty-five years of conditioning, if you forget what you really want to do, what you really want to be, it is only natural.

The first thing to decide is whether there is a deep longing in you to know the truth. Are you ready to risk everything for it, even your life if the need arises? If it is so, "Then," Ko Hsuan says, "...these words are for you." If you are only a worldly person—by "worldly" he means one who is interested in money, power, prestige—then it would be better if you don't bother about such great things. They are not for you—at least, not yet. First you have to become fed up with all your worldly desires. Go into those desires. Unless you become tremendously frustrated, unless you see that they are all futile—that whether you succeed or fail you always fail; that whether you have money or you are poor you are always poor; that whether you are a beggar or an emperor you are always a beggar...when that insight dawns on you, only then can you become a seeker of the beyond. Otherwise, if you pretend to be a seeker of the beyond, you will bring your whole world with you, you will bring all your desires with you.

That's why people think of God, of heaven. It is not that they are interested in God and heaven; they are only interested in power and prestige. Maybe they are afraid of death, and out of fear and greed they start praying to God. But a prayer that arises out of fear and greed is not prayer at all. A real prayer arises out of gratitude, never out of fear and greed. A real prayer arises out of love for truth, whatsoever it may be. Otherwise, your worldly desires will again be projected onto God, onto heaven.

If you compare the descriptions of paradise in different religions and different countries, you will be surprised: what they desire is projected. For example, the Tibetan paradise is described as warm—obviously, because

Tibetans suffer from the cold so much that they would like heaven to be full of sun and warmth so that they can at least take a bath every day. In Tibet the scriptures say that it is your duty to take a bath at least once a year!

The Indian paradise is cool, air-conditioned. They did not know about air-conditioning at that time so it is described as "air-cooled." It is bound to be so—India has suffered so much from the heat, all the Indian mind wants is a little shade and coolness. So the Indian paradise is always full of cool breezes and there are big trees, so big that a thousand bullock carts can rest under a single tree. The Indian idea is of heaven is shade and coolness.

The Tibetan hell is absolutely icy and the Indian hell is full of fire. Now, there cannot be so many hells and so many paradises: these are our projections. Whatever we desire we project onto heaven and whatsoever we are afraid of we project onto hell. Hell is for others, for those who don't believe in our ideology, and paradise is a reward for those who do believe in our ideology—it is the same worldly mind. These are not religious people.

In the Mohammedan heaven there are streams of wine. This is very strange. Here you condemn wine—it is a sin—and there you reward your saints with wine?

All the paradises of all the cultures are full of beautiful women because the ideas of paradise are created by men. I have never come across a description of beautiful men. If women someday write about paradise, they won't talk about beautiful women, they will talk about beautiful men, men always following the women like shadows, obedient, just like servants! That's how women have been painted by men in their heaven.

And the women are always young; they never grow old. This is strange! If you look at the idea of God, all the religions think of God as a very old man. Have you ever thought of God as a young man? No country has ever thought of God as a young man because you cannot trust young people: they are dangerous and a little foolish, too. A wise man has to be old, so God is very old. But the women he is surrounded with are all very young—in fact, stuck at the age of eighteen; they don't grow beyond that. Stagnant! They must be getting tired of remaining eighteen for millions of years. But this is a man's idea. Here the saints renounce women, they renounce sex; they condemn sex, they praise celibacy—and, of course, they are hoping they will be paid well: they will be rewarded with beautiful young women in heaven.

These are our worldly desires coming from the unconscious; you cannot push them away. Unless you have encountered them, unless you have watched them, you cannot just repress them.

Ko Hsuan is right. He says, "The worldly cannot understand it." They are bound to misunderstand.

The new patient comes into the analyst's office. He is a theologian, a great scholar, and a philosopher. He says, "Doctor, I came here because everybody says I think too much of myself."

"Let's get into this," says the doctor. "To analyze your problem it is necessary that you

tell me your story; it is necessary that you tell me your problem from the very beginning."

"Okay," says the professor, and sitting down, he continues. "In the beginning all was darkness…"

You see? He really begins from the very beginning! His understanding is bound to remain with him wherever he goes, whatever he does. Whatever he chooses is going to be out of his mind and mentality. How long can you repress? How long can you hide? It is going to come up, if not from the front door, then from the back door.

Two madmen in an asylum look at the clock: it is twelve o'clock.

One says, "It is midday."

The other says, "It's midnight."

The discussion becomes so heated that they decide to ask the director. "Is it midday or midnight, sir?" they ask him.

The director looks at his watch and says, "Well, I don't know—my watch has stopped."

In a madhouse, you can't expect the director to be less mad than the madmen. In fact, he may be the director because he is more mad! He may be the oldest inmate; hence, he has been chosen to be the director.

Ko Hsuan says in his preface: "I received these words from the divine ruler of the Golden Gate."

Truth is always a gift; it is not an achievement, because all achievements belong to the ego and truth cannot be part of your ego trip. Truth happens only when the ego is dropped, so you cannot say, "I have achieved it," you can only say, "It has been given. It is a

doing for centuries and what masters have been instructing their disciples to do. Empty yourself, become a nothingness, and the moment you are absolutely nothing, at that very moment, truth descends in you—you become full of it. First you have to be empty of yourself and then you become full of God, Tao, Dharma, or whatever name you choose to call it.

Ko Hsuan says, "I received it from the divine ruler of the Golden Gate." This is a mysterious saying, "the Golden Gate." That is the Taoist way of saying that God is not a person but a gate, an opening into existence. If you are empty, the door opens *within you*. It is your ego that is blocking the door; it is *you* who are blocking the door; except for you, there is no hindrance. Remove yourself, don't stand between, and suddenly the Golden Gate opens. It is called "golden" because the moment you pass through it, you are pure gold. The dust disappears, is transmuted, is transformed; it becomes divine.

This is the definition of alchemy: transforming dust into the divine, transforming base metal into gold. And it happens simply by becoming a receiver. You have to be utterly a nonentity.

Ko Hsuan says, "It has been previously only transmitted by word of mouth. Those who will be able to comprehend the meaning will become ambassadors of the divine and enter the Golden Gate."

This small preface says, "Those who will be able to comprehend it, understand it, will become ambassadors of the divine...." Not that they *have to* become, they will become—

gift." Ko Hsuan is right. He says, "I received it..."

Remember: you have to be at the receiving end. You are not to be aggressive about truth. The real seeker is not an achiever. The real seeker is not aggressive, is not masculine.

When you are a real seeker you become feminine. You are like a womb—you receive. You empty yourself completely, so that space is created to receive. That's the whole art of meditation, and that's what mystics have been naturally, without any effort, effortlessly. They *will* start radiating godliness, they will start radiating light, and they will become luminous. Miracles will happen through them without any effort.

It is said that many miracles happened in Ko Hsuan's life. They are the same miracles that have been happening to many mystics. For example, it is said that he was able to walk on water. The same is said about Jesus. It is not a fact, remember—Jesus is not so foolish neither is Ko Hsuan so foolish; as to walk on water. There is no need to walk on water. Then what does it mean? It is a poetic expression; it is a metaphor. It means they were able to do the impossible. And what is the most impossible thing in the world? The most impossible thing in the world is to transcend the world. The most impossible thing in the world is to know oneself. The most impossible thing in the world is to become utterly empty.

This is a metaphor: "walking on water." Don't take it as fact. It is a poetic way of saying something.

The second thing said about Ko Hsuan is that he knew the secret of the elixir of life, the secret of alchemy. One who knows his consciousness—the consciousness that is a witness to his thoughts—one who comes to know his state of no-mind, knows absolutely that there is no death for him. No birth, no death—he knows that he has never been born and will never die; he has gone beyond both. This is the secret of life; this is the secret science of alchemy.

The third thing said about Ko Hsuan is that he ascended to the beyond in the full light of day. That is said about Mohammed also, and about many others. These are all beautiful ways of expressing the inexpressible. These people have ascended to the ultimate, but not by any back door; they have achieved to the ultimate in the full light of the day. Those who had eyes have seen them ascending. Those who had ears have heard the music when they were ascending. Those who had hearts to feel have felt their transformation. These people lived on the earth and yet they belonged not to the earth. They were not earthly people; they were utterly unearthly.

Don't be misguided by religious fanatics who insist that these metaphors are not metaphors but facts, that these poetic expressions are not poetic expressions, but part of history. Be a little more poetic if you really want to understand the mystic way of life.

The perfection of paradise was such that Peter got bored. One day, when everyone was sitting all together, he said to God, "I am so bored...I'd love to visit earth now and then, wouldn't you?"

"Not at my age," replies God.

Says Jesus, "Once has been enough for me."

Says the Holy Ghost, "Not until they stop shooting at doves!"

Jesus is called by his Father, who tells him that he has to sacrifice himself once more for the redemption of mankind.

Though rather unwillingly, Jesus agrees to go.

He goes around heaven saying goodbye to all his friends and promising to come back in thirty-three years. Then, followed by all the angels, he comes down to earth.

Thirty-three years go by, but there is no sign of Jesus. Finally, after eighty years, a lean old man comes to heaven saying that he is Jesus. He is taken to God, who recognizes him immediately and exclaims in astonishment, "What happened? Why did you take so long?"

"Well, you see, Father," replies Jesus, "… there is no more capital punishment on earth, so I was condemned to a life sentence!"

Jesus is walking among the people and performing miracles. Suddenly a man falls at his feet and says, "Lord, Lord, cure me, cure me!"

"Calm down, son. Have faith and you will be cured."

Jesus moves closer to the man and looks into his eyes, then backs away and signals to Peter to come over. As Peter draws near, Jesus whispers to him, "It's not going to work, Peter. Pretend we have to go—he's got cancer!"

Reality is reality!

Either these miracles are metaphors or some coincidence. For example, Lazarus coming back to life—he may have been in a coma. Or it may be just a beautiful metaphor, because every master calls his disciple to come back to life from his grave. Ordinarily, you are dead; you have not tasted of life at all. You are all Lazaruses! And Lazarus was dead for only four days; everybody has been dead for millions of lives. It would certainly be a miracle to call you forth! And if you listened and came back to life it would be just as much

a miracle done by you as it would be a miracle done by the master. In fact, you will be doing a greater miracle than the master!

The same miracles are described in all the lives of the saints; there are not many differences for the simple reason that every mystic lives such a life that he is in the world and yet not in the world. How to express it? How to say something significant about him? It can be said only through miracles. The language of miracles is the only possible way to express something, at least to hint at something, that is indescribable.

But there are foolish people who cling to these things and then start creating an account of history. They are not helpful in spreading the divine message; they create obstacles and hindrances. In fact, many more intelligent people would be with Jesus if all these miracles and the nonsense attached to them were dropped. Yes, fools would desert him because they are only with him because of the miracles, but intelligent people would be with him.

Sometimes coincidences happen and sometimes a series of coincidences can make a person believe. When these things happen—and these things can happen, it is such a vast world—people are bound to believe. People are gullible. But there are no miracles. There is only one miracle—*the* miracle—and that is your being utterly empty. The death of the ego is the only miracle; if that happens you have passed through the Golden Gate. You have known what eternity is; you have gone beyond time.

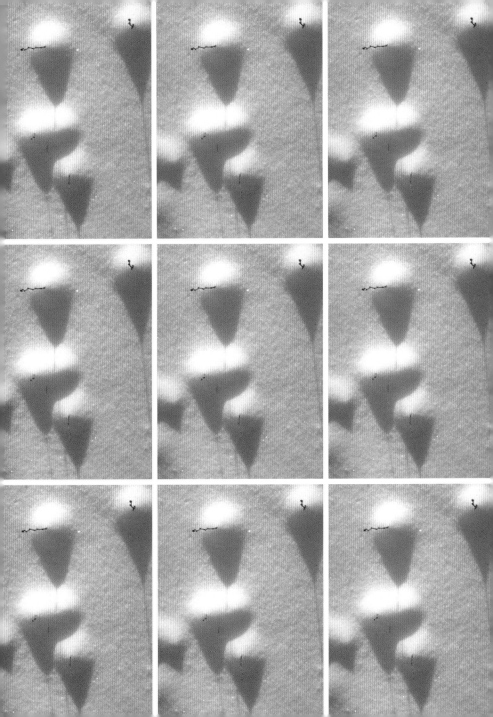

Now these small verses of Ko Hsuan:
The venerable master said,
"The supreme Tao is formless…"

From the beginning, Ko Hsuan wants you to know that Tao has no form, so you cannot make a statue of Tao, you cannot create a temple around Tao, you cannot create rituals; no priesthood is possible.

The supreme Tao is formless; it is the universal law of existence. You cannot worship it and you cannot pray to it. All your worship is foolish and all your prayers are unheard and will remain unheard. There is nobody to hear your prayers or to fulfill your prayers. Your prayers are your desires in a new form. Watch your prayers—see what they are. The garb is religious, the jargon is religious, but nothing has changed; the desires are the same. People are asking for money, power, prestige. Whatever you are asking for, you are asking for something wrong, because there is nobody to give you anything. The very idea of receiving by asking is absurd. Be utterly silent.

Tao is not the path of prayer. It is the path of meditation.

"…Tao is formless, yet it produces and nurtures heaven and earth."

It does not mean that Tao is indifferent to you; it simply means you cannot worship it, you cannot pray to it. But it nourishes you, it nurtures you. The whole breathes it. It is the heartbeat of the cosmos, but not a person.

"The supreme Tao has no desires…"

If you want to have a communion with Tao, you will have to drop all desires. People change their desires, but they basically remain the same. People change their outer structures of life: they call it "character." Somebody smokes, you may not smoke, you start chewing gum. It is the same stupidity. Or you may stop chewing gum and start doing something else. But because you are the same, nothing is going to change. If you go to the moon, you will do the same things that you are doing here. Everything will be different and nothing will be different.

A human couple has been captured by aliens from Mars and is taken to the living room of the flying saucer. They are greeted by a Martian couple, offered green drinks, and begin chatting. After several drinks, everyone relaxes. The man from Earth asks the Martians, "How do you procreate?"

"My wife and I will demonstrate for you," answers the Martian.

The Martians go over to a refrigerator-like closet and the female picks up a bottle containing brown liquid and the male picks up a bottle containing white liquid. They go over to a table where there is an empty jar. Each pours the liquid into the empty jar.

"Now we put the jar in this closet," explains the Martian, "and in nine months we will have another baby. How do you do it on Earth?"

So the Earth couple demonstrates for the Martians. They take off their clothes and lie down on the floor with the man on top of the woman. As they are coming and going, they notice the Martians are laughing at them.

"What are you laughing at?" they ask.

"Excuse us," they answer, "…but we find it very funny because that is the same way we make coffee!"

You can be here, you can be on the moon, you can be on Mars, you can change outer things—it makes no difference. Either you will make love in a stupid way or you will make coffee in a stupid way, but you will do something stupid unless intelligence arises in you, unless your unconsciousness is transformed into consciousness, unless your darkness disappears and becomes light.

The supreme Tao has no desires yet by its power the sun and moon revolve in their orbits. The supreme Tao is nameless, yet it ever supports all things. I do not know its name...

These are immensely valuable words: "I do not know...." That's how the people who know speak. The people who claim that they know are utterly ignorant. The real knower functions out of a state of not knowing.

Ko Hsuan says, *I do not know its name... but for title call it Tao.*

We have to call it something. Note the non-fanatic attitude. You can call it anything—XYZ. Tao simply means XYZ. Because we have to call it something, we call it Tao. If you choose some other name, there is no problem.

When Buddhists reached China they were surprised because Taoist mystics agreed with them. They said, "Perfectly right! We call it Tao; you call it Dharma. It is the same thing, because we define Tao as nameless and you define Dharma as nameless. We say Tao is formless and you say Dharma is formless, so there is no problem. We are only speaking different languages, but we are indicating the same truth."

That is one of the most beautiful things that has ever happened in history. When Buddhism

THE PRACTICAL WAY

Tao does not believe in miracles; it believes in scientific methods to transform your life.

Lao Tzu, Chuang Tzu, and Lieh Tzu were walking together along a forest path one day when they came upon a fast-flowing river that barred their way. Immediately Lieh Tzu sat down on the bank of the river and meditated upon the eternal Tao. Ten minutes later he stood up and proceeded to walk on the water to the other side.

Next, Chuang Tzu sat in the lotus posture for twenty minutes, whereupon he stood up and also walked across the river.

Lao Tzu, watching this in amazement, shrugged his shoulders, sat down on the riverbank like the others and meditated for over an hour. Finally, with complete trust in the Tao, he closed his eyes, took one step into the river, and fell in.

On the other shore, Chuang Tzu laughed, turned to Lieh Tzu and said, "Should we tell him where the rocks are?"

Tao does not believe in any nonsense. It is very pragmatic, practical, and down to earth.

reached China there was no conflict, no argumentation, no conversion, yet Buddhists and Taoists met and mingled and became absolutely one. It has not happened in the history of Christianity or Judaism or in the history of Mohammedanism: their history is full of ugliness. It has happened only in the tradition of Buddha and Lao Tzu. A very rare phenomenon—no argumentation. They simply tried to understand each other and they laughed and hugged and they said, "Perfectly true!"

A Christian missionary went to see a Zen master, and he started reading the beatitudes from the Bible. He said, "Blessed are the meek for theirs is the kingdom of God."

The Master said, "Stop! That's enough. Whoever has said it is a buddha."

The missionary was utterly dumbstruck. He had come to argue; he had come to convert; he had come to convince the Zen master that Buddha was wrong and Jesus was right. And this man said, "Whosoever has said it—I don't know who has said it—but whosoever has said it is a buddha. There is no need to read more; that one sentence is enough. You can taste the ocean from anywhere, it tastes the same—it is salty. This one sentence will do!"

The same happened in China. Buddhists arrived and the whole of China became Buddhist without anybody converting anybody else. Because Taoism was so generous and Buddhism was so understanding; there was no question of converting anybody. The whole idea of converting anybody is ugly, violent.

They never argued—yes, they communed, they nodded at each other's understanding, and they said, "Yes, that's true. That's what Lao Tzu also says. That's what Buddha has said in his own words." And out of this meeting—which is the rarest in the whole of humanity—Zen was born. Out of the meeting of Buddha and Lao Tzu, out of the meeting of Buddha's insight and Taoist insight, out of the meeting of Dharma and Tao, Zen was born. Hence, Zen is a rare flowering. Nowhere else has it happened that way—so silently, without bloodshed, without a single argument. There was no question of argument; the difference was only of language.

This is how a truly religious person is. He is not a fanatic—he cannot be.

Ko Hsuan says:

I do not know its name but for title call it Tao.

It is a nameless experience, but we have to call it something so we will call it Tao. That is arbitrary. If you have some other name—God, Logos, Dharma, Truth, Nirvana—you can choose from those names; they are all beautiful. Because it has no name of its own, any name will do.

This approach should be our approach. We should not be part of any dogma—Christian, Mohammedan, Hindu. We should not belong to any church; that is all childish, political. A religious person is absolutely free from all dogma. Only in freedom understanding grows.

Understand this approach toward life; this is fundamental. Once you are rooted in it you will start growing. Great foliage will happen to you and great flowering and fulfillment.

about the author

Osho (1931–1990) is a contemporary mystic whose teachings have inspired millions of people from all walks of life. His works, which are published in more than 40 languages, are transcribed from extemporaneous talks given over a period of 35 years. They cover everything from the individual search for happiness to the most pressing social, political, and spiritual concerns of our time. *The Sunday Times* of London has named Osho as one of the "1000 Makers of the 20th Century." His books are bestsellers in many languages and many countries. Other books by Osho on Tao include:

Tao: The Pathless Path When the Shoe Fits (Chuang Tzu)
Tao: The Three Treasures (Four volumes on Lao Tzu)
The Empty Boat (Talks on the stories of Chuang Tzu)
The Secret of Secrets: Secret of the Golden Flower Meditation—The First and Last Freedom
For the availability of editions in different languages check the Osho website.

"He quotes Jesus, Buddha, Mahavira, Lao Tzu, Sufis, and old Zen masters with stupendous memory, interpreting them with a freshness and directness as if they were speaking today, as if they wore jeans "
Die Zeit, Germany

"Osho is one of the most remarkable orators I have ever heard."
BERNARD LEVIN, *The Times*, UK

OSHO INTERNATIONAL WEBSITE
For more information see: www.osho.com—a comprehensive website in several languages with information about the author, his work, and the Osho International Meditation Resort.